About Phonics Connection:

Welcome to RBP Books' Connection series. Like our Summer Bridge Activities™ collection, this series is designed to make learning fun and rewarding. Connection Phonics books are based on the premise that mastering language skills builds confidence and enhances a student's entire educational experience. A fundamental factor in learning to read is a strong phonics foundation, beginning with an awareness of the alphabet, understanding phonemic relationships and the concept of words, and moving on to word recognition. This workbook is based on core curriculum and is designed to reinforce classroom phonics skills and strategies. Pages include graphics, examples, and simple directions to introduce phonics concepts such as letter and sound recognition, word families, long and short vowels, blends, sight words, beginning and ending sounds, contractions, plurals, prefixes and suffixes, antonyms and synonyms, homophones, and silent letters. Phonics Connection books also provide writing practice.

This phonics workbook is a plan for reading and writing success! It was built to encourage students at the third grade reading level, giving them direct phonics practice, writing and reading comprehension exercises, as well as test-taking skills to prepare them for standardized testing.

The **five sections** found on the workbook pages are as follows:

Direct Activity—gives immediate and direct experience with the concept.

Writing Practice—students practice forming complete sentences in diverse ways by writing poetry, short stories, commercials, tongue twisters, definitions, songs, jokes, and more. Not only does this make writing fun and interesting, but it draws on the student's own experiences to encourage writing success!

Test-Taking Skills—practice with types of question and answer formats found on standardized tests for better, smarter test-taking.

Integrated Activity—a creative supplement that provides phonics connections with various subjects like math, science, social studies, social skills, etc. Perfect for homework or classroom lesson extension activities!

Core Curriculum Concept—outlines for the teacher and parent the concepts and skills being covered. It also allows for easy notation/inclusion in respective lesson plans.

New concepts are briefly described at the top of the page and clear examples are given.

Sections are brief to make the work go faster. Phonics skills are repeated in various ways so the student will be able to perfect them without tiring from doing too much of the same kind of activity.

Sample answers are provided to show the students what to do so they can proceed on their own.

Reading and Writing pages are filled with humorous stories and comprehension questions to entertain while increasing reading comprehension capabilities.

Every page also has a possible point value that adds up to twenty. This allows students to easily gauge their own level of understanding, giving them ownership over their learning. (If the use of these sheets for grading purposes is desired, the number of twenty points lends easily to grade/point value conversion tables.)

Reviews of concepts are built into games like crossword puzzles, word searches, mazes, mystery messages, dot-to-dots, and more! Students will learn and love it!

Dear Parents and Educators,

Thank you for choosing this Rainbow Bridge Publishing educational product to help teach your children and students. We take great pride and pleasure in becoming involved with your educational experience. Some people say that math will always be math and reading will always be reading, but we do not share that opinion. Reading, math, spelling, writing, geography, science, history, and all other subjects will always provide some of life's most fulfilling adventures and should be taught with passion both at home and in the classroom. Because of this, we at Rainbow Bridge Publishing associate the greatness of learning with every product we create.

It is our mission to provide materials that not only explain, but also amaze; not only review, but also encourage; not only guide, but also lead. Every product contains clear, concise instructions, appropriate sample work, and engaging, grade-appropriate content created by classroom teachers and writers that is based on national standards to support your best educational efforts. We hope you enjoy our company's products as you embark on your adventure. Thank you for bringing us along.

Sincerely,

George Starks
Associate Publisher
Rainbow Bridge Publishing

Phonics Connection™ • Grade 3
Written by Hollie Hendricks

Illustrations
Amanda Sorensen

Visual Design and Layout
Andy Carlson, Robyn Funk, Zachary Johnson, Scott Whimpey

Publisher
Scott G. Van Leeuwen

Editorial Director
Paul Rawlins

Associate Publisher
George Starks

Copy Editors and Proofreaders
Elaine Clark, Suzie Ellison, Linda Swain, Esther Yu

Series Creator
Michele Van Leeuwen

Technology Integration
James Morris, Dante J. Orazzi

Please visit our website at
www.summerbridgeactivities.com
for supplements, additions, and corrections to this book.

First Edition 2003

For orders call 1-800-598-1441
Discounts available for quantity orders

ISBN: 1-932210-25-3

PRINTED IN THE UNITED STATES OF AMERICA
10 9 8 7 6 5 4 3 2 1

Phonics - Grade 3
Table of Contents

Beginning Sounds

Direct Activity

Write the word for each picture. Circle the **beginning sound**. (2 points each.)

1.

b̶a l l

2.

_ _ _ _ _ _

3.

_ _ _ _ _ _

Writing Practice

Write a word that begins with the same **beginning sound** as the picture. Circle the beginning sound. Then write a sentence using that word. Circle that word in the sentence. (2 points each.)

1.   ⓙungle _____

At the zoo we saw all kinds of (jungle) animals. _____

2.   _____

_____

3. _____

_____

Test-Taking Skills

Fill in the circle beside the correct **beginning sound**. (2 points each.)

1.
   - Ⓐ s
   - Ⓑ f
   - Ⓒ l
   - Ⓓ y
   - Ⓔ none

2.
   - Ⓐ o
   - Ⓑ n
   - Ⓒ d
   - Ⓓ t
   - Ⓔ none

3.
   - Ⓐ w
   - Ⓑ s
   - Ⓒ e
   - Ⓓ h
   - Ⓔ none

4.
   - Ⓐ a
   - Ⓑ k
   - Ⓒ g
   - Ⓓ u
   - Ⓔ none

Integrated Activity

Choose a picture from this page. Circle all the words with the same **beginning sound** that you can find on a page from the newspaper.

> Core Curriculum Concept: Identification of words with initial consonants, sound-symbol association with initial consonants, and use of these words in context.

Ending Sounds

Direct Activity

Write the word for each picture name. Circle the ending sound. (2 points each.)

1.

f l a (g)

2.

_ _ _

3.

_ _ _ _

Writing Practice

For each number, write the word for the picture. Then write a sentence using that word. Circle that word in the sentence. (2 points each.)

1. book(k)

My favorite (book) is Superfudge by Judy Blume.

2. _____

_____

3. _____

_____

Test-Taking Skills

Fill in the circle beside the correct **ending sound**. (2 points each.)

1.
Ⓐ h
Ⓑ d
Ⓒ i
Ⓓ n
Ⓔ none

2.
Ⓐ h
Ⓑ m
Ⓒ a
Ⓓ b
Ⓔ none

3.
Ⓐ g
Ⓑ l
Ⓒ s
Ⓓ a
Ⓔ none

4.
Ⓐ c
Ⓑ a
Ⓒ p
Ⓓ t
Ⓔ none

Integrated Activity

Cut out pictures from an old grocery store ad. Place all of the pictures with the same ending consonant sound together and glue them in groups on a piece of paper. Have a friend try to guess what each group has in common.

> Core Curriculum Concept: Identification of words with final consonants, sound-symbol association with final consonants, and use of these words in context.

Initial Consonant Digraphs: *sh*, *wh*, *ch*, *th*, and *thr*

Some consonants that are put together stand for a single sound. These are called **consonant digraphs** (or consonant pairs). **Sh**, **wh**, **ch**, **th**, and **thr** are examples of common consonant digraphs found at the beginning of words.

Direct Activity

Write the word that goes with each picture. Circle the **digraph** in each word. (2 points each.)

1.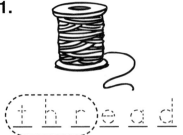

t h r e a d

2.

_ _ _ _ _

3.

_ _ _ _ _ _ _

Writing Practice

For each **digraph** listed below, write a word using that digraph. Then use that word in a sentence. Circle the digraphs. (2 points each.)

1. sh short _____ Our cat is short compared to our dog. _____

2. th _____ _____

3. ch _____ _____

Test-Taking Skills

Say the picture name. Fill in the circle beside the correct **consonant digraph** found in the picture name. (2 points each.)

1.
   - Ⓐ sh
   - ⬤ ch
   - Ⓒ wh
   - Ⓓ th
   - Ⓔ none

2.
   - Ⓐ sh
   - Ⓑ ch
   - Ⓒ thr
   - Ⓓ wh
   - Ⓔ none

3.
   - Ⓐ wh
   - Ⓑ ch
   - Ⓒ sh
   - Ⓓ th
   - Ⓔ none

4.
   - Ⓐ wh
   - Ⓑ thr
   - Ⓒ th
   - Ⓓ ch
   - Ⓔ none

Integrated Activity

Open a drawer, cupboard, or your fridge and list all the things you see with **consonant digraphs** in their names.

> Core Curriculum Concept: Identification of words with initial consonant digraphs **sh**, **wh**, **ch**, **th**, and **thr**, sound-symbol association with initial consonant digraphs, and use of those words in context.

Ending Consonant Digraphs: *ch*, *tch*, *ng*, *sh*, and *th*

Consonant digraphs (or consonant pairs) can also be found at the end of words like in the word *lunch*. Other examples of consonant digraphs found at the end of words are **tch**, **ng**, **sh**, and **th**.

Direct Activity

Finish the word that goes with each picture. Circle the **digraph** in each word. (2 points each.)

1.

t r a (s h)

2.

m o u _ _

3.

r i _ _

Writing Practice

For each **digraph** listed below write a word using that digraph. Then use that word in a sentence. Circle all the digraphs in the sentence. (2 points each.)

1. ch crun(ch) _____   I like (th)e way potato (ch)ips crun(ch) in my mou(th). _____

2. ng _____   _____

3. th _____   _____

Test-Taking Skills

Say the picture name. Fill in the circle beside the correct **consonant digraph** sound in the picture name. (2 points each.)

1. Ⓐ ch
Ⓑ ng
Ⓒ sh
Ⓓ th
Ⓔ none

2. Ⓐ th
Ⓑ ch
Ⓒ sh
Ⓓ ng
Ⓔ none

3. Ⓐ ng
Ⓑ sh
Ⓒ tch
Ⓓ th
Ⓔ none

4. Ⓐ th
Ⓑ sh
Ⓒ tch
Ⓓ ng
Ⓔ none

Integrated Activity

On a blank paper, write a **consonant digraph** in big letters. Paint over the entire page with watercolors. Before the paint dries, sprinkle salt along the pencil lines as you say the **digraph** sound. Watch what happens.

> Core Curriculum Concept: Identification of words containing final consonant digraphs **ch**, **tch**, **ng**, **sh**, and **th**, sound-symbol association with final consonant digraphs, and use of those words in context.

Consonant Digraphs: *gh* and *ph*

The **consonant digraphs** (or pairs) **gh** and **ph** make the \f\ sound when they are found together in words.

Direct Activity

Match the word to each picture. Circle the **digraphs** in each word. (2 points each.)

1.

phone
graph
tough

2.

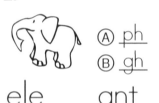

cough
photo
enough

3.

alphabet
telephone
telegraph

Writing Practice

Choose a word with a **gh** or **ph** digraph in it and write it on the top line. This will be your poem title. Write a four-line rhyming poem on the lines below using the word you chose. (6 points.)

Tough
It is tough
To think of stuff
That rhymes with "ough."
How about enough!

Test-Taking Skills

Write the correct **digraph** to complete each word in the spaces below. Then, fill in the circle beside that digraph. (2 points each.)

1.

Ⓐ ph
Ⓑ gh

nep h ew

2.

Ⓐ ph
Ⓑ gh

ele __ __ ant

3.

Ⓐ ph
Ⓑ gh

lau __ __

4.

Ⓐ ph
Ⓑ gh

__ __ ase

Integrated Activity

Write **gh** or **ph** in the middle of a piece of paper. Draw pictures of all the things you can think of with that **digraph** in their names.

> Core Curriculum Concept: Identification of words containing consonant digraphs **gh** and **ph**, sound-symbol association with consonant digraphs, and use of those words in context.

Consonant Digraph Mix: *ch, sh, th, tch, wh, ng, ph, gh,* and *thr*

Direct Activity

Find the word that matches the picture and put a line through it. Next, find the **digraph** in that word and write it in the blanks below. (2 points each.)

1.

s h

chip ~~dish~~

2.

___ ___

tough

3.

___ ___

stitch throw

Writing Practice

Finish the silly story on the lines below. Use at least six words with **consonant digraphs**: *ch, sh, th, tch, wh, ng, ph, gh, thr*. Circle all the digraphs in your story. (6 points.)

I wish this elephant could throw enough string to catch a
spaceship. Then I could... _____

_____

_____

_____

_____

Test-Taking Skills

Fill in the circle next to the **consonant digraph** that would correctly complete the word.
(2 points each.)

1. ___ite
Ⓐ th
Ⓑ ch
● wh
Ⓓ thr
Ⓔ none of these

2. ___oat
Ⓐ thr
Ⓑ sh
Ⓒ gh
Ⓓ wh
Ⓔ all of these

3. ___ack
Ⓐ ch
Ⓑ sh
Ⓒ th
Ⓓ ph
Ⓔ C & D only

4. swi___
Ⓐ ng
Ⓑ sh
Ⓒ tch
Ⓓ A, B & C
Ⓔ none of these

Integrated Activity

Word-Scotch—Use ten words with **consonant digraphs** to fill in the boxes of a hopscotch board, one word for each number. Say the word you want the marker to land on. When the marker lands on that square, make up a sentence using the word and complete your turn.

Core Curriculum Concept: Identification of words containing consonant digraphs **ch, sh, th, tch, wh, ng, ph, gh,** and **thr,** sound-symbol association with consonant digraphs, and use of those words in context.

Two-Letter Blends: blends with *t*, *s*, *p*, and *g*

When two or three consonants are found together in a word, they form a **blend**. To say the blend, put the letter sounds together, such as the **sq** blend in *squirt*.

Direct Activity

Write the **two-letter blend** found in each picture. (2 points each.)

1.
   t r

2.
   __ __

3.
   __ __

Writing Practice

Make a word by adding a **two-letter blend** of your choice to the endings below. Write that word in a sentence and circle all the blends. (2 points each.)

1. t rail   The (sl)ippery (tr)ail leads to a (pl)ace with a (str)eam.

2. __ __ain   _____

3. __ __ack   _____

Test-Taking Skills

Fill in the circle next to the correct **blend**. (2 points each.)

1.
   - (A) sn
   - (B) pl
   - (C) gr
   - (D) tr
   - (E) none

2.
   - (A) pr
   - (B) gl
   - (C) st
   - (D) tr
   - (E) none

3.
   - (A) sl
   - (B) pr
   - (C) gr
   - (D) tr
   - (E) none

4.
   - (A) pr
   - (B) gl
   - (C) sn
   - (D) tr
   - (E) none

Integrated Activity

Make as many **two-letter blend** words as you can with pasta or cereal letters. Glue the words onto a piece of construction paper.

Core Curriculum Concept: Identification of words containing two-letter consonant blends, use of those words in context, and sound-symbol association of consonant blends with: **t, s, p,** and **g**.

Two-Letter Blends: blends with *c*, *f*, and *b*

Direct Activity

Write the correct **two-letter blend** for the picture. (2 points each.)

1.
c r

2.
__ __

3.
__ __

Writing Practice

Write a new word that has the same **two-letter blend** as the picture below. Use that word in a sentence. Circle the blends. (2 points each.)

1. (fl)ying _____ I saw a (fl)ag (fl)ying in the south wind.

2. _____ _____

3. _____ _____

Test-Taking Skills

Say the picture name. Fill in the circle beside the correct **two-letter blend** sound in the picture name. (2 points each.)

1.
Ⓐ fr ●
Ⓑ cl
Ⓒ br
Ⓓ sn
Ⓔ none

2.
Ⓐ br
Ⓑ cl
Ⓒ fr
Ⓓ fo
Ⓔ none

3.
Ⓐ bl
Ⓑ cr
Ⓒ sn
Ⓓ cl
Ⓔ none

4.
Ⓐ cr
Ⓑ fl
Ⓒ fo
Ⓓ fr
Ⓔ none

Integrated Activity

Find all the book titles in your library with **two-letter blends** in them. List the words you found.

Core Curriculum Concept: Identification of words containing two-letter consonant blends, use of those words in context, and sound-symbol association of consonant blends with: **c**, **f**, and **b**.

Three-Letter Blends: *spr*, *scr*, *spl*, and *str*

Sometimes s will be placed in front of a two-letter blend, forming a **three-letter blend**. To say the blend, add the s sound to the front, as in **s** + **cr** in *scream*.

Direct Activity

Write the correct **s blend** for each picture. (2 points each.)

1.

2.

3.

1. s t r

2. _ _ _

3. _ _ _

Writing Practice

Make a word by writing the **three-letter blend** in the blanks below. Use each word in a sentence and circle the s blends. (2 points each.)

1. s c r eam   When I get angry I feel like I want to scream.

2. _ _ _ ay   _____

3. _ _ _ ap   _____

Test-Taking Skills

Fill in the circle above the correct **three-letter blend** that completes the word in each sentence. (2 points each.)

1. As I was running outside I s p r ained my ankle.

   Ⓐ Ⓑ Ⓒ Ⓓ
   spr scr str spl

2. Today I helped my dad _ _ _ ew the shelf into the wall.

   Ⓐ Ⓑ Ⓒ Ⓓ
   spr scr spl str

3. My favorite desserts are banana _ _ _ its!

   Ⓐ Ⓑ Ⓒ Ⓓ
   spr scr str spl

4. A new kid moved in just down the _ _ _ eet.

   Ⓐ Ⓑ Ⓒ Ⓓ
   spr scr str spl

Integrated Activity

Look through a recipe book and list all the **three-letter s blends** you can find.

Core Curriculum Concept: Identification of words containing three-letter consonant blends, use of those words in context, and sound-symbol association of three-letter consonant blends with **s**.

www.summerbridgeactivities.com   Phonics—Grade 3—RBP0253

Ending Blends: *st, nd, mp, ft*, etc.

When two consonants appear at the end of a word, say the sounds of each letter and blend them together. Like **nd** in the word *friend*.

Direct Activity

Draw a line from the picture to the correct **ending blend**. (2 points each.)

1.    **2.**   **3.**

lf   mp   sk   ft   ft   nk   sk   lp   mp   ld   sk   nd

Writing Practice

For each **ending consonant blend**, write a sentence using that blend as many times as you can. Circle all of the ending consonant blends. (2 points each.)

1. lt   Wa(lt) bui(lt) a be(lt) with fe(lt).

2. mp _____

3. nk _____

Test-Taking Skills

Fill in the circle next to the word with an **ending consonant blend** that fits the clue.
(2 points each.)

1. a large body of water
     Ⓐ park   Ⓑ pond   Ⓒ lake   Ⓓ tub

2. part of your hand
     Ⓐ finger   Ⓑ palm   Ⓒ thumb   Ⓓ B and C

3. a baby horse
     Ⓐ kid   Ⓑ pony   Ⓒ mule   Ⓓ colt

4. something you might wrap for a birthday
     Ⓐ stamp   Ⓑ craft   Ⓒ gift   Ⓓ box

Integrated Activity

Write down as many words with **ending consonant blends** as you can. Count them and record the number on the back. Fill in the spaces in between the words with letters. See if you or a friend can find all of the hidden words with ending consonant blends on the page.

> Core Curriculum Core: Identification of words containing ending consonant blends, use of those words in context, and sound-symbol association of ending consonant blends such as **st**, **nd**, **mp**, **ft**, etc.

Short Vowel Sounds: ă

Direct Activity

Write the word for each picture. Circle the **short a** vowels. (2 points each.)

1.

h (a) t

2.

— — — —

3.

— — — — — —

Writing Practice

Pick any **short a** word you'd like and write it on the top line. This will be your poem title. Make up a poem using that word and other short *a* words and write it on the lines below. Circle all of the short *a* vowels. (6 points.)

Cat

This crazy cat

has just sat

on that man's hat.

Can you imagine that?

Test-Taking Skills

Fill in the circle that is found below a **short a** word in each sentence.

(2 points each.)

1. "It is time to <u>take</u> my <u>bath</u>!" said <u>Tracy</u>.
               Ⓐ   ●   Ⓒ   Ⓓ   Ⓔ none of these

2. My <u>pal</u> <u>Mazy</u> likes to <u>bake</u> <u>cakes</u> and muffins.
       Ⓐ   Ⓑ   Ⓒ   Ⓓ   Ⓔ none of these

3. <u>Today</u> I found an ancient <u>map</u> of <u>Australia</u> in our <u>basement</u>.
     Ⓐ   Ⓑ   Ⓒ   Ⓓ   Ⓔ none of these

4. The best <u>treats</u> are <u>cupcakes</u> with <u>candies</u> and <u>chocolate</u> on top.
          Ⓐ   Ⓑ   Ⓒ   Ⓓ   Ⓔ none of these

Integrated Activity

Cut out pictures of **short a** words from old magazine pages. Glue the pictures onto a piece of paper to make a short *a* collage.

> Core Curriculum Concept: Identification of words containing the **short a** vowel sound and use of those words in context.

www.summerbridgeactivities.com   Phonics—Grade 3—RBP0253

Short Vowel Sounds: ĕ

Direct Activity

Write the word for each picture. Circle the **short e** vowels. (2 points each.)

1.

ⓔg̲g̲

2.

— — — —

3.

— — — — —

Writing Practice

Make up two riddles using as many **short e** words as you can. Circle all the short *e* vowels. (3 points per riddle.)

What do you gⓔt
whⓔn you put an
ⓔlⓔphant and a
squirrⓔl togⓔther?
Answer: A trunk full
of nuts.

_____
_____
_____
_____
Answer: _____
_____

_____
_____
_____
_____
Answer: _____
_____

Test-Taking Skills

Fill in the circle that is found below a **short e** word in each sentence. (2 points each.)

1. Last <u>week</u> <u>we</u> went camping and <u>set</u> up a <u>tent</u>.
   Ⓐ   Ⓑ   Ⓒ   Ⓓ   ● C & D

2. There are <u>three</u> new <u>people</u> in our pie–<u>eating</u> <u>contest</u>.
          Ⓐ   Ⓑ   Ⓒ   Ⓓ   Ⓔ none of these

3. I <u>held</u> the door open for <u>Uncle</u> <u>Steve</u> and <u>he</u> thanked me.
     Ⓐ   Ⓑ   Ⓒ   Ⓓ   Ⓔ none of these

4. On <u>Tuesday</u> I <u>wrote</u> a <u>letter</u> to my <u>niece</u>, Emily.
      Ⓐ   Ⓑ   Ⓒ   Ⓓ   Ⓔ A & C

Integrated Activity

Write as many **short e** words as you can with bubbles and a bubble wand. Have a friend try to guess the words. (You may want to do this activity outside.)

> Core Curriculum Concept: Identification of words containing the **short e** vowel sound and use of those words in context.

Phonics—Grade 3—RBP0253

www.summerbridgeactivities.com

©RBP Books

Short Vowel Sounds: ĭ

Direct Activity

Write the word for each picture. Circle the **short i** vowels. (2 points each.)

1.

2.

3.
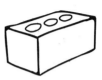

s t (i) c k

_ _ _ _ _

_ _ _ _ _ _

Writing Practice

Write **short i** words on the lines below. Next to each word write a clue that describes the short *i* word. (2 points each.)

1. _____ wig _____   a rug made of hair you can wear on your head

2. _____   _____

3. _____   _____

Test-Taking Skills

Fill in the circle next to the **short i** word that names the picture. (2 points each.)

1.
Ⓐ ice
Ⓑ igloo
Ⓒ house
Ⓓ sit

2.
Ⓐ sink
Ⓑ paint
Ⓒ lid
Ⓓ ink

3.
Ⓐ hole
Ⓑ lid
Ⓒ mitt
Ⓓ fall

4.
Ⓐ shed
Ⓑ grind
Ⓒ mill
Ⓓ hill

Integrated Activity

Make a **short i** "Word Pizza." Write down all the short *i* words you can think of on paper strips of different shapes and different colors. Then glue them onto a brown paper circle.

> Core Curriculum Concept: Identification of words containing the **short i** vowel sound and use of those words in context.

Short Vowel Sounds: ŏ

Direct Activity

Write the word for each picture. Circle the **short o** vowels. (2 points each.)

1.

m ⓞ p

2.

— — — — — — — —

3.

— — — — — —

Writing Practice

Finish the silly story below by adding at least six of your own **short o** words. Circle all the short *o* words. (2 points each.)

Bob the monster had a frog named Molly that liked to jog and...

_____

_____

_____

_____

Test-Taking Skills

Fill in the circle next to the **short o** word that names the picture. (2 points each.)

1.
   Ⓐ open
   Ⓑ knock
   Ⓒ lock
   Ⓓ look

2.
   Ⓐ stone
   Ⓑ rock
   Ⓒ stop
   Ⓓ roll

3.
   Ⓐ log
   Ⓑ pig
   Ⓒ mitt
   Ⓓ fall

4.
   Ⓐ switch
   Ⓑ light
   Ⓒ lot
   Ⓓ off

Integrated Activity

Make a list of all the **short o** words you can think of. Draw a picture illustrating all those words. See if a friend can find all the short *o* things in the picture.

> Core Curriculum Concept: Identification of words containing the **short o** vowel sound and use of those words in context.

Short Vowel Sounds: ŭ

Direct Activity

Write the word for each picture. Circle the **short u** vowels. (2 points each.)

1.

n (u) t

2.

_ _ _

3.

_ _ _ _

Writing Practice

Make a word by adding letters to the beginning of the **short u** endings. Use the word in a sentence and circle all of the short *u* sounds. (2 points each.)

1. f̲un   I have so m(u)ch f(u)n chewing b(u)bble g(u)m! _____

2. __ump   _____

3. __um   _____

Test-Taking Skills

Fill in the circle below the **short u** word in each sentence. (2 points each.)

1. This <u>blue</u> stone brings <u>luck</u> when I play a <u>tune</u> on my <u>flute</u>.
   Ⓐ   Ⓑ   Ⓒ   Ⓓ   Ⓔ B and D

2. For <u>lunch</u> I had a <u>cup</u> of <u>soup</u> with <u>blueberry</u> jam on toast.
   Ⓐ   Ⓑ   Ⓒ   Ⓓ   Ⓔ A and B

3. The <u>unicorns</u> we saw were <u>running</u> <u>from</u> a <u>mule</u>.
   Ⓐ   Ⓑ   Ⓒ   Ⓓ   Ⓔ B and D

4. A <u>mouse</u> picked <u>up</u> each <u>crumb</u> of bread <u>under</u> the table.
   Ⓐ   Ⓑ   Ⓒ   Ⓓ   Ⓔ B, C and D

Integrated Activity

See how many **short u** words you can spell using toothpicks. List them on a piece of paper.

> Core Curriculum Concept: Identification of words containing the **short o** vowel sound and use of those words in context.

www.summerbridgeactivities.com   Phonics—Grade 3—RBP0253

Short Vowel Sounds: ă, ĕ, ĭ, ŏ, ŭ

Direct Activity

Write the word for each picture. (2 points each.)

1.

   c u p

2.

   _ _ _ _ _

3.

   _ _ _ _ _

Writing Practice

Choose a word that uses the short vowels listed below. Use that word in a sentence and circle all of the same short vowels. (2 points each.)

1. ĕ ___set___ On Wednesday night it's Ellen's job to set the table.

2. ŭ _____ _____

   _____

3. ĭ _____ _____

   _____

Test-Taking Skills

Fill in the circle next to the word that names the picture. (2 points each.)

1.
   Ⓐ pup
   Ⓑ hill
   ⬤ pot
   Ⓓ bet

2.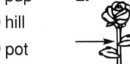
   Ⓐ kit
   Ⓑ plan
   Ⓒ flop
   Ⓓ stem

3.
   Ⓐ bit
   Ⓑ bat
   Ⓒ but
   Ⓓ bop

4.
   Ⓐ rabbit
   Ⓑ dog
   Ⓒ hen
   Ⓓ kitten

Integrated Activity

Write all the short vowel words you can think of on strips of paper. Put the strips in a bag. With a friend, take turns choosing a word and acting it out. Take turns trying to guess the word.

> Core Curriculum Concept: Identification of words containing short vowel sounds and use of those words in context.

Phonics—Grade 3—RBP0253   www.summerbridgeactivities.com   ©RBP Books

Reading and Writing with Short Vowels

Read the short story below and then answer the questions.

The Little Puddle Duck

Pat the duck had a habit of puddle hopping. She loved to jump from puddle to puddle singing and whistling all the way. Pat loved walking in big puddles. She loved stepping into little puddles. She loved skipping in short puddles, and she especially loved stomping into long puddles. The long puddles splashed the best, making smaller puddles all around so there were more puddles for Pat! By the time Pat got home she was very wet! Pat's mom was not happy when she saw Pat all wet and muddy and dripping on the rug. "Hmmmmmm," said Pat's mom. "A hat for Pat! That's the plan!" And with that she got a slick red hat that would stop Pat from getting wet and dripping all over the rug. When Pat saw her new red hat she was so glad! "Ah ha!" said Pat, "Now I can splash without getting wet and muddy!" And with that, a very happy Pat went to splash and splash in the fresh puddles.

Fill in the circle next to the sentence that tells the main idea or what this story is mostly about. (1 point.)

1. Ⓐ   a mother duck who wants to buy a hat for her baby duck
    Ⓑ   a beautiful new red hat
    Ⓒ   a little duck who loves to jump into puddles
    Ⓓ   very large puddles

Core Curriculum Concept: Identification and decoding of words containing short vowel sounds and use of those words in context.

Reading and Writing with Short Vowels

2. In a complete sentence, write what happened in the story to make Pat's mom decide to buy her a hat. (1 point.)

_____

_____

3. Using complete sentences, write what kinds of puddles Pat liked to jump into the best and why. (2 points.)

_____

_____

_____

4. Using complete sentences, write about what the hat did for Pat and how she felt about getting the hat. (2 points.)

_____

_____

_____

5. Below each letter, list two words from the story with short vowel sounds. (10 points.)

ă	ĕ	ĭ	ŏ	ŭ
hat	_____	_____	_____	_____
_____	_____	_____	_____	_____

6. List four words from the beginning of the story that tell what Pat loved to do in puddles. (4 points.)

_____   _____

_____   _____

Long Vowel Sounds: ā

Direct Activity

Write the word for each picture. Circle the **long a** vowel in each word. (2 points each.)

1. s n (a) k e

2. _ _ _ _

3. _ _ _ _ _ _ _ _

Writing Practice

Choose a **long a** word and write it on the top line. This will be your poem title. Then write a five-line rhyming poem on the lines below using long *a* words. Circle all the long *a* sounds in each line. (6 points.)

C(a)kes

When I aw(a)ke

I like to b(a)ke

A pile of panc(a)kes

And on top I m(a)ke

A syrup l(a)ke.

_____

_____

_____

_____

_____

_____

Test-Taking Skills

Fill in the circle next to the **long a** word that makes sense in each sentence below. (2 points each.)

1. When will we _____ the dog for a walk?
   - Ⓐ talk 🅑 take Ⓒ tan Ⓓ ten

2. For Halloween Mom made my little brother a Superman _____.
   - Ⓐ net Ⓑ cake Ⓒ can Ⓓ cape

3. When the firemen arrived they quickly put out the _____.
   - Ⓐ garbage Ⓑ flakes Ⓒ flames Ⓓ dog

4. The ocean _____ broke against the cliffs.
   - Ⓐ waves Ⓑ shells Ⓒ wade Ⓓ boat

Integrated Activity

Make a crossword puzzle using as many **long a** words as you can.

Core Curriculum Concept: Identification of words containing the **long a** vowel sounds and use of those words in context.

www.summerbridgeactivities.com
Phonics—Grade 3—RBP0253

Long Vowel Sounds: ā

Direct Activity

Draw a picture of each **long a** word. (2 points each.)

1.

state

2.

face

3.

grapes

Writing Practice

Finish this story using at least six **long a** words. Put a box around the long *a* words. (6 points.)

Drake the snake tried to make cupcakes but found that he was out of...

_____

_____

_____

_____

Test-Taking Skills

Fill in the circle below the **long a** word in each sentence. (2 points each.)

1. Can you tell Stanley that I had to go.
   Ⓐ   Ⓑ   Ⓒ   Ⓓ   ● none of these

2. We are all going to take turns riding on Dan's bike.
      Ⓐ   Ⓑ   Ⓒ   Ⓓ   Ⓔ none of these

3. James wants to drive to the lake with Blane and Dane.
   Ⓐ   Ⓑ   Ⓒ   Ⓓ   Ⓔ all of these

4. Baggy the ape loves to snack on bananas.
   Ⓐ   Ⓑ   Ⓒ   Ⓓ   Ⓔ all of these

Integrated Activity

Write the letter *a* in the middle of a chalkboard. With a partner take turns adding letters, one at a time, to the letter *a* until someone finishes a **long a** word. Give that person a point. Erase the board and start a new round. After eleven rounds, the winner is the one with the most points.

Core Curriculum Concept: Identification of words containing the **long a** vowel sound and use of those words in context.

Long Vowel Sounds: ā

Direct Activity

Draw a line to the correct name of each picture. Put a box around all of the **long a** vowels.
(2 points each.)

1.

m⬜ke
m⬜ne
mall
man

2.

tap
take
tan
tape

3.

lane
land
lake
lad

Writing Practice

Make a word by adding letters to the beginning of each **long a** ending. Use that word in a sentence and put a triangle around it. (2 points each.)

1. pane   The baseball hit the window and broke the pane.

2. __ake

3. __ame

Test-Taking Skills

Fill in the circle next to the **long a** ending that completes the word. (2 points each.)

1. s_____
- Ⓐ afe
- Ⓑ and
- Ⓒ it
- Ⓓ ack
- Ⓔ none of these

2. fl_____
- Ⓐ ap
- Ⓑ an
- Ⓒ ate
- Ⓓ ake
- Ⓔ none of these

3. pl_____
- Ⓐ ant
- Ⓑ an
- Ⓒ ane
- Ⓓ unk
- Ⓔ none of these

4. g_____
- Ⓐ as
- Ⓑ ab
- Ⓒ ate
- Ⓓ ap
- Ⓔ none of these

Integrated Activity

Look around the room and write down all of the objects that can be described with **long a** words.

Core Curriculum Concept: Identification of words containing the **long a** vowel sound and use of those words in context.

Long Vowel Sounds: ā

Activity

Find at least twenty **long a** words and circle them in the word search below. (There are over seventy words in all.)

```
e s a c p h c c p x t e x p r q r r t r r i b w f e l x n e l c
e x b k i s a s w q c r x e b b t z e z q b x e o a r e c w f s
w s b a s e a s f a w s e e j n q z m g g c a s k t k a q w a c
k c a m a l e k r i k n r n p z a i t d t a x c l a p e m a t m
w n j h y y i c e s a l e a q r a l r w a g m j b e u x v k e f
h h r c n w j p l t a w r c w n e n z l e v c c d h q k e r c
d e g a r r o v e e o h n c a k s f z e e e c a l p o b p a v z
a j z w a s s j r h g f s k t t n e b h k s r b h f r a m v y y
r b e n g b k r a s p n e v a f k k b e j t s a a m c e k a m t
a i g p h a s e l a c w a t n e n a r t z p r k a r p p r u z m
r e h g x p t k f n f r e h i j e u y a k e j n a p e d f y l e
e c w w b a l e p e r a r t c k n q i t d l e t z t q e w d s e
c e l h d p n v f m r a v e a e m h h u s a f e t r e s g s v k
a k a a w u l a y t u x r c w k d t r e r a c s t s p c n a i a
x a t l c z n a a w p c l i z j e r o f d o n z p d a a b e e l
w r e e a f k m n a i u w o z c g a e n a c f a e e k p k l e f
h y z p c a e v d e k p b v a g z e j e x a c k m e p e a p q w
a u h a r c j e q k h c n r m d l v v m t e a k r e b a a m l o
t s u h h e t s a t n a b v r l z a c u u t i a e m g t x s w n
e a v s a r r a n g e k w g a w r n f w s o c d b l c k h e k s
y s f e p j f a m e f e z k e c y s o c j j f y o o s a g e p x
q l y o o a d m f y k y e h x v z v m o h g g d n r b p v a l b
```

Write the words you find on the lines below. (20 points.)

_____ _____ _____

_____ _____ _____

_____ _____ _____

_____ _____ _____

_____ _____ _____

_____ _____ _____

_____ _____

> Core Curriculum Concept: Identification and decoding of words containing the **long a** vowel sound.

Long Vowel Sounds: ī

Direct Activity

Write the word for each picture. Circle the **long i** vowel in each word. (2 points each.)

1.

w r (i) t e

2.

_ _ _ _

3.

_ _ _ _

Writing Practice

Choose a **long i** word and write it on the top line below. This will be your poem title. Write a five line rhyming poem using long *i* words. Circle all of the long *i* sounds in each line. (6 points.)

Mike

Mike really likes

To ride his bike,

A three-wheel trike.

Even when he hikes

He takes his bike.

_____

_____

_____

_____

_____

_____

Test-Taking Skills

Fill in the circle below the **long i** word that makes sense in each sentence. (2 points each.)

1. The job I like most is wiping the windows on the building.
   Ⓐ   Ⓑ   Ⓒ   Ⓓ   ● Ⓔ A and B

2. Bill's wife, Jill, has a job prescribing pills.
   Ⓐ Ⓑ Ⓒ   Ⓓ   Ⓔ none of these

3. Even when it's chilly in April the windowsill tulips still bloom.
   Ⓐ   Ⓑ   Ⓒ Ⓓ   Ⓔ none of these

4. I like to write lines of poetry and carve them with a knife.
   Ⓐ   Ⓑ   Ⓒ   Ⓓ   Ⓔ all of these

Integrated Activity

Make a valentine for someone using as many **long i** words as you can!

Core Curriculum Concept: Identification of words containing the **long i** vowel sound and use of those words in context.

Long Vowel Sounds: ī

Direct Activity

Write the word for each picture. Circle the **long i** vowel in each word. (2 points each.)

1.

p (i) n e

2.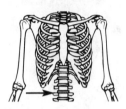

_ _ _ _ _

3.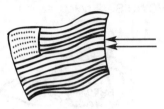

_ _ _ _ _ _

Writing Practice

Finish the silly story using at least six **long i** words. Put a line under all the long *i* words.
(6 points.)

On Vine Street five hungry mice lived in a pile of pine needles...

_____

_____

_____

_____

_____

Test-Taking Skills

Fill in the circle below the **long i** word in each sentence. (2 points each.)

1. The old silver mine on the hill was filled with dust.
   Ⓐ ⬤Ⓑ   Ⓒ   Ⓓ   Ⓔ A and B

2. How much time does it take to read a dictionary?
              Ⓐ   Ⓑ   Ⓒ   Ⓓ   Ⓔ none of these

3. Nikki said the snake would be sticky and slimy, but it wasn't.
   Ⓐ   Ⓑ   Ⓒ   Ⓓ   Ⓔ none of these

4. Sometimes when I hike up wide cliffs I can see for miles.
   Ⓐ   Ⓑ   Ⓒ   Ⓓ   Ⓔ all of these

Integrated Activity

Make up a song using as many **long i** words as you can. Sing it to someone.

> Core Curriculum Concept: Identification of words containing the **long i** vowel sound and use of those words in context.

Long Vowel Sounds: ī

Direct Activity

Draw a line to the correct **long i** name of each picture. Put a rectangle around all the long *i* vowels. (2 points each.)

1.

note
valent[i]ne
card
n[i]ce

2.

rice
soup
slice
cereal

3.

lines
twine
animals
mice

Writing Practice

Make a word by adding letters to the beginning of each **long i** ending. Use that word in a sentence and circle it. (2 points each.)

1. bite   Don't put your fingers in the bird's cage because she will (bite).

2. __ice   _____

3. __ine   _____

Test-Taking Skills

Fill in the circle next to the **long i** ending that completes the word. (2 points each.)

1. str_____
Ⓐ eam
Ⓑ ing
● ipe
Ⓓ ice
Ⓔ none of these

2. tw_____
Ⓐ ice
Ⓑ ipe
Ⓒ in
Ⓓ ip
Ⓔ none of these

3. wh_____
Ⓐ ice
Ⓑ ite
Ⓒ ere
Ⓓ en
Ⓔ none of these

4. tr_____
Ⓐ ip
Ⓑ im
Ⓒ ine
Ⓓ ike
Ⓔ none of these

Integrated Activity

Cut out pictures of **long i** words from an old magazine and make a long *i* collage by gluing the pictures onto a piece of paper.

> Core Curriculum Concept: Identification of words containing the **long i** vowel sound and use of those words in context.

©RBP Books   www.summerbridgeactivities.com   Phonics—Grade 3—RBP0253

Long Vowel Sounds: ī

Activity

Find at least twenty **long i** words and circle them in the word search below. (There are over seventy words in all.)

```
s d c k j u e t v o s g c p p a p h e b n k s c x x n u a y p s
i p v f i f e n l f x q l r i g i q c g j x r z v s l i c e e z
d o s s t c o e c i f q i a l h l n i e i t b u i d r j f p r q
e a u e j s q b e v l c a g v k e v r c n z z l c r s i l y i k
l s n b v f u s h e e e v a y t s e h i o w d l e d h e t h f w
i e s i p i i r k f n h l f u o f e t p o m e i c u i c c h q y
h d h r x r n t p i t e d h k k w b d s d n s p v c n v v i u e
w i i t h y i e l r n g l q k n o r e e i e i e f i e p i p m c
q e n j d m c j t t i x w o r e i m i h q c z k c w d m k n x i
g t e c u b e x i y c s r t z x i f s t s i e i a p s e i w e r
e i p o i m n n z m i t e i t r h n e t e x e r w b b r q r s y
l r k t p e e s z n y n l a g p o k b q c s e t h m t d q w c q
i p e i r f j s l o i a i n i o m u h j i r u s i k z o i l f k
m s d i i y e w u i e n b e m b i u z r i t s b l v p n i r n c
s j w w b c t l m r m m v j r g l x a t a z u e e f e m p f t r
o c k b i g e w i w k e f i e i e a o x b c v s k k e d d i e w
e b y r y e y n i t h g v g t x h i n s i d e v e i j w m c i c
b v p f g l k a i c x i x f c e h s m n x x f d l c l e i n p j
i z i o e e h u p m e r t s l c c e s i w l p a r f i t e h g f
k b c h p i q v k u c q t e e t c w p c b k c r n i e d z r r v
e c i l p s i e s r i i a j u c c o n f i d e m i c v z e w c o
d c s g b l e m i d l l l w n n l r k x h i r e x t f e i c v k
```

Write the words you find on the lines below. (20 points.)

_____   _____   _____

_____   _____   _____

_____   _____   _____

_____   _____   _____

_____   _____   _____

_____   _____   _____

_____   _____   _____

> Core Curriculum Concept: Identification and decoding of words containing the **long i** vowel sound.

Long Vowel Sounds: ō

Direct Activity

Write the **long o** word for each picture. Put a rectangle around the long *o* vowel in each word. (2 points each.)

1.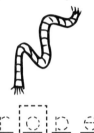

r o p e

2.

— — — — —

3.

— — — —

Writing Practice

Choose a **long o** word and write it on the top line below. This will be your poem title. Write a five-line rhyming poem about that word using long *o* words. Put a rectangle around all the long *o* words in each line. (6 points.)

Mole

The sad mole

Was in a hole

He called his home,

He was all alone

With just his phone.

_____

_____

_____

_____

_____

_____

Test-Taking Skills

Fill in the circle next to the **long o** word that makes sense in each sentence below. (2 points each.)

1. Don't _____ around the house, find something to do!
   - Ⓐ rope
   - 🅑 mope
   - Ⓒ cope
   - Ⓓ hope

2. The Olympic swimmer _____ into the pool so gracefully.
   - Ⓐ jumped
   - Ⓑ hole
   - Ⓒ fell
   - Ⓓ dove

3. Someone _____ from the cookie jar when all they had to do was ask.
   - Ⓐ took
   - Ⓑ stole
   - Ⓒ store
   - Ⓓ more

4. Is the earth's _____ a solid or liquid?
   - Ⓐ crust
   - Ⓑ dust
   - Ⓒ shore
   - Ⓓ core

Integrated Activity

Finger paint all of the **long o** words that you can think of with pudding on waxed paper. You can lick your fingers when you're done!

Core Curriculum Concept: Identification of words containing the **long o** vowel sound and use of those words in context.

www.summerbridgeactivities.com   Phonics—Grade 3—RBP0253

Long Vowel Sounds: ō

Direct Activity

Draw a picture of each **long o** word. (2 points each.)

1.   2.   3.

home   hole   cone

Writing Practice

Finish the silly story using at least six **long o** words. Put a circle around all the long *o* words. (6 points.)

One (lonely) (cowpoke) (drove) out on the range looking for a (home)...

_____

_____

_____

_____

Test-Taking Skills

Fill in the circle below the **long o** word in each sentence. (2 points each.)

1. I <u>hope</u> the <u>flock</u> of geese <u>stops</u> to rest on their way <u>south</u>.
   Ⓐ   Ⓑ   Ⓒ   Ⓓ   Ⓔ A and B

2. My favorite <u>flowers</u> are <u>roses</u> and <u>poppies</u> but I also like <u>olive</u> trees.
                Ⓐ   Ⓑ   Ⓒ   Ⓓ   Ⓔ none of these

3. We <u>drove</u> to the <u>store</u> <u>before</u> going to the <u>shore</u>.
      Ⓐ   Ⓑ   Ⓒ   Ⓓ   Ⓔ all of these

4. There are <u>more</u> <u>cookies</u> on the <u>front</u> shelf by the soda <u>pop</u>.
             Ⓐ   Ⓑ   Ⓒ   Ⓓ   Ⓔ all of these

Integrated Activity

Write a letter to your hero using as many **long o** words as possible.

> Core Curriculum Concept: Identification of words containing the **long o** vowel sound and use of those words in context.

Long Vowel Sounds: ō

Direct Activity

Draw a line to the correct **long o** name for each picture. Put a rectangle around all the long *o* vowels. (2 points each.)

1.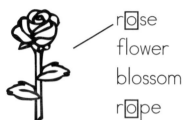

r□se
flower
blossom
r□pe

2.

nose
notes
point
not

3.

cope
cream
con
bone

Writing Practice

Make a word by adding letters to the beginning of each **long o** ending. Use that word in a sentence and circle it. (2 points each.)

1. <u>wr</u>ote   I (wrote) all about the amazing trip in my journal.

2. __ope   _____

3. __one   _____

Test-Taking Skills

Fill in the circle next to the **long o** ending that completes the word. (2 points each.)

1. st_____
Ⓐ ore
Ⓑ ope
Ⓒ ole
Ⓓ one
🅔 A, C, and D

2. p_____
Ⓐ ole
Ⓑ one
Ⓒ ote
Ⓓ ove
Ⓔ none of these

3. al_____
Ⓐ ote
Ⓑ ope
Ⓒ oke
Ⓓ one
Ⓔ none of these

4. h_____
Ⓐ oke
Ⓑ ope
Ⓒ ole
Ⓓ ote
Ⓔ B and C

Integrated Activity

Air Writing—Using your finger, write **long o** words in the air. Take turns guessing and writing with a friend.

> Core Curriculum Concept: Identification of words containing the **long o** vowel sound and use of those words in context.

Long Vowel Sounds: ō

Activity

Find at least twenty **long o** words and circle them in the word search below. (There are over seventy words in all.)

```
m m v k l e t d s a k t t p t m t q s g s c o n e n q h c b x e
q q k b s o e t k o u y r o e o p v n x u t l b w l s e s o r h
b i a o w l o t g u x a s s n r e q c z p g n s t o n e a o f e
l p n z o l a t o t e t w e r x o w n d p b k a t h p c g e n t
l h l p e d h p r l s n s d w o s n c l o y o n p h m b n o n i
t u y i o y s a s b e l k g z o v s s f s i b n c v k o h o j x
a a e v f u h p e e s c r u l p e e h p e v y w e t h p t r q e
m e e d b v p o e m p t h e s o p o u o a a p o v p a e e s o h
j c c p r o p o s e o o o o n r o p m l r o q x e x e n r f b s
n e p o r f e c f d l r r k k e l m i e k e z l a o n o h c t y
i e e e x z l j n v b h x l e e s g v e j c e s h o o l z w k s
w h r n u m o l e h f e o o x k g y n p o t p y y f b c n h t v
a m o o c e h j r w x f v m a k o e t e k e f x r s m c m o z n
q c m h o o n v g g p z y o e l q x x l e u f o o y o u r x g g
a l o p y v v o w g n o m e l l w s j o x d z l y e r e w o e n
z y u o u a k e t n e v x v x c o w i h e e e n f l t l j x b t
o y e l a h q e f s u o q k r d o c a t n s z y z o t s w k m e
r o c y s v j y r e y e d z a c o o g o g l o v e r s e t o n g
e m q x o x v w w o e n c o r e h w e p y v j r p c u a p o r s
p e r o f e b f o z t c e r o h c o k o s y q r a w b o z t v u
o t d k a z o s p r m a e z x d j u s n t a l o n e r w h h s e
r a w l c j p h r z e p h u e r o c p e x x z n e b o l r a e l
```

Write the words you find on the lines below. (20 points.)

_____   _____   _____

_____   _____   _____

_____   _____   _____

_____   _____   _____

_____   _____   _____

_____   _____   _____

> Core Curriculum Concept: Identification and decoding of words containing the **long o** vowel sound.

Phonics—Grade 3—RBP0253   www.summerbridgeactivities.com   ©RBP Books

Long Vowel Sounds: ū

Direct Activity

Write the word for each picture name. Put a triangle around the **long u** vowel in each word.
(2 points each.)

1.

f l u t e

2.

＿ ＿ ＿ ＿

3.

＿ ＿ ＿ ＿

Writing Practice

Choose a **long u** word and write it on the top line below. This will be your poem title. Write a five line poem using long *u* words and put a triangle around them. (6 points.)

Mute

A very cute

And happy newt

Sang no tune

In the month of June

Because it was mute

Test-Taking Skills

Fill in the circle below the **long u** word that makes sense in each sentence below. (2 points each.)

1. Did you know that a _____ makes music?
   - Ⓐ lute
   - Ⓑ dune
   - Ⓒ drum
   - Ⓓ thumb

2. The _____ is a winter Olympic event.
   - Ⓐ tumble
   - Ⓑ luge
   - Ⓒ chute
   - Ⓓ fluke

3. An inch is a unit of _____.
   - Ⓐ flute
   - Ⓑ cute
   - Ⓒ measure
   - Ⓓ secure

4. When I asked Dad if I could go, he said _____.
   - Ⓐ sure
   - Ⓑ yes
   - Ⓒ okay
   - Ⓓ nope

Integrated Activity

Write a comic strip using **long u** words for the characters' names. Look at the funnies section of a Sunday paper for some ideas. Share it with a friend.

> Core Curriculum Concept: Identification of words containing the **long u** vowel sound and use of those words in context.

Long Vowel Sounds: ū

Direct Activity

Draw a picture of each **long u** word. (2 points each.)

1.

mule

2.

tube

3.

huge

Writing Practice

Finish this short story using at least six **long u** words. Circle all of the long u words. (6 points.)

The (cute) (Duke) loved (music,) but the only thing he could (use) to play a (tune) was his (juke) box...

_____

_____

_____

Test-Taking Skills

Fill in the circle below the **long u** word in each sentence. (2 points each.)

1. Last <u>August</u> I got <u>stuck</u> with the <u>mumps</u>, but now I'm <u>immune</u>.
   (A)　　　　　(B)　　　　　(C)　　　　　●(D)　(E) none of these

2. A <u>muddy</u> <u>truck</u> ran through the <u>muck</u> and got <u>stuck</u>.
   (A)　(B)　　　　　(C)　　　(D)　　(E) none of these

3. In <u>summer</u> there are lots of sand <u>dunes</u> that are <u>fun</u> to <u>run</u> on.
   (A)　　　　　　　　　　(B)　　　(C)　(D)　(E) none of these

4. Last night I went to <u>brush</u> my teeth <u>but</u> the <u>tube</u> was <u>out</u> of toothpaste.
   (A)　　　(B)　(C)　(D)　(E) all of these

Integrated Activity

Draw a picture filled with things that have the **long u** sound in their names. Cut it into pieces to make a puzzle and try to put it back together!

Core Curriculum Concept: Identification of words containing the **long u** vowel sound and use of those words in context.

Long Vowel Sounds: ū

Direct Activity

Draw a line to the correct **long u** name of each picture. Put a triangle around all the long *u* vowels. (2 points each.)

1.

fire
f△se
△se
t△ne

2.

mule
measure
inches
sure

3.

flute
rude
mule
lute

Writing Practice

Make a word by adding letters to the beginning of each **long u** ending. Use that word in a sentence and circle it. (2 points each.)

1. truce   The soldiers on both sides called for a (truce) to end the war.

2. __ute   _____

_____

3. __ure   _____

_____

Test-Taking Skills

Fill in the circle next to the **long u** ending that completes the word. (2 points each.)

1. s_____
- Ⓐ ube
- Ⓑ ule
- Ⓒ ure
- Ⓓ uce
- Ⓔ none of these

2. m_____
- Ⓐ ute
- Ⓑ uce
- Ⓒ ube
- Ⓓ ule
- Ⓔ A and D

3. fl_____
- Ⓐ ute
- Ⓑ ube
- Ⓒ uce
- Ⓓ ule
- Ⓔ none of these

4. d_____
- Ⓐ ule
- Ⓑ upe
- Ⓒ uke
- Ⓓ ube
- Ⓔ C and D

Integrated Activity

Draw a map of a pretend town, and name all of the streets using **long u** words. Take turns with a friend giving directions and walking down the "streets" with your fingertips.

> Core Curriculum Concept: Identification of words containing the **long u** vowel sound and use of those words in context.

Long Vowel Sounds: ū

Activity

Find at least twenty **long u** words and circle them in the word search below. (There are over seventy words in all.)

```
p c p y g w a d o k q j e g i p w f w j h x j e r u p m i n s z
v e l y q d u i j p v l j d n a t u r e c e y h b c e q f c b y
r g l d a h d s x m r c w z u n u r b a q t k x x u l t u j m u
e w s u s v m t a f o u u q w d f i i b i v i r q c t e u b u x
t u u y m e e n u g y z n l x n r o c i n u a e e q e q d l t v
u a s r h s i s t u b a e e t e r u s j e n m d h m v c p c e u
c l t u u c e e z e b b c h h u r s y e u u u r u j r q q y u u
u j e f u n x s h t s e m u f f r g n l s r i s p u n c t u r e
b q n r h r c r g u f k b l u e e e g i c d s p a u e a r e e q
e o e n v o t u i l p s p s c g s s c r i a j z u g p s v s u e
c f c f r e u p f f t i r e p u s i u c u c u u v h n s e u s r
j k b d s o r o z r u z c v t e a a u f g l u e k e u u n c e p
u c x v p u r u d d a d e t y n m l q s e n e r k e p r u c v b
z e u c f t o m t x m t d e u o e l f e i r q z e u b e t a v e
i r u p u i u i r p r q u c u r u h o c j g a s f w d o d s w l
v u q n i g n q r u a r r i x r e e y o e r u t u f f c x c m u
g s e f x d i r e u g c m r e f d c p i s m h u g e f f g l y y
u n r c h z v a v t c c m p x a l q o d a i m e a s u r e u l i
e u u i g w e k f r a c t u r e d e n u j t q l d h u e c e c z
b u l s c w r v s j s c u l p t u r e t c o u w u h o f a r e c
y n e u a b s r q v e n u d n b w t i s r a t l b g i m m u n e
a z r m q i e w d i p u t s x y d d x y d u d g b n e c q p w z
```

Write the words you find on the lines below. (20 points.)

_____   _____   _____

_____   _____   _____

_____   _____   _____

_____   _____   _____

_____   _____   _____

_____   _____

Reading and Writing with Long Vowels

Read the short story below, and then answer the questions.

An Ice Maze

Jake, Blake, and Dane awoke to see nine white flakes of snow land outside their windowpanes. "Nice!" yelled Blake. He wrote his name on the frosted pane and raced to the phone to tell Jake and Dane to ride their bikes over to his home. "If we take our time and stay inside a while, there will be huge piles of white snow and ice later to make a maze!" Jake said to Blake. So they went to hide in a place and make pictures of the maze they were aching to trace in the ice and snow. By five o'clock it was late enough to find piles of the white flakes outside. "It's time to brave the freezing cold! Let's go!" The boys dove in the snow. They forged holes all over the yard making tubes of ice that curved and snaked. "More," said Dane. "We need more holes for the maze." So the boys waded through the snow making more slopes until their faces and toes were frozen and sore. Jake, Blake, and Dane forged to the driveway when the neighbors, James and Rose, came over to stare at the scene. "What are you making?" James blared. The boys turned pale. They were amazed. "Can't you see?" Jake asked. "It's an ice maze." "Looks like a lot of huge snow piles to me," James remarked. "You're crazy! We've traced in the ice all day!" Blake said.

"Well," said James. "Maybe you'd like to go ice-skating with Rose and me. We're making piping hot chocolate later." The boys thought about it and agreed that making the maze was amusing, but they wanted a change, and skating was a fine idea. "Besides, I could sure use a nice cup of piping hot chocolate!" said Dane. The three of them agreed. So, all five friends—Blake, Jake, Dane, Rose, and James—rode their bikes to the lake and skated until late. Making the maze turned out to be a good excuse to play in the snow, and ice-skating was a super way to close the day!

> Core Curriculum Concept: Identification and decoding of words containing long vowel sounds and use of those words in context.

Reading and Writing with Long Vowels

1. Fill in the circle next to the sentence that best tells the main idea of the story. (1 point.)

  Ⓐ Three boys make a new friend.
  Ⓑ While building a maze three boys learn it's okay to try new things.
  Ⓒ Three boys learn to skate.
  Ⓓ Three boys begin the day by building a maze but end up skating with friends.

2. In a complete sentence write what happened in the story that made the boys decide to go skating. (1 point.)

_____

_____

3. Using complete sentences, write what the boys' plan for the day was and how it changed. (2 points.)

_____

_____

4. Using complete sentences, write what the neighbor said about the ice maze and how the boys felt about what he said. (2 points.)

_____

_____

5. Below each matching letter, list two words with long vowel sounds that were used in the story. (10 points.)

ā	ē	ī	ō	ū
Jake				

6. List the four long vowel words from the story that tell what the boys did in the snow. (4 points.)

_____   _____

_____   _____

Sounds of Y: long *e* sound (ē)

A **y** at the end of a word usually makes the **long e** sound if the word has other vowels in it. The word *candy* is a good example.

Direct Activity

Below each picture write *yes* if **y** makes the **long e** sound or *no* if it does not make the **long e** sound. (2 points each.)

1.
family

_____yes_____

2.
fry

_____

3.
pretty

_____

Writing Practice

Read the words below. If the **y** ending makes the **long e** sound, circle it. If the **y** ending does not make the **long e** sound, put an X through it. Use each word in a sentence and put a rectangle around it. (2 points each.)

1. (story)   I wrote a [story] about a dog and a horse. _____

2. sunny   _____

3. my   _____

Test-Taking Skills

Fill in the circle next to the word *yes* if the **y** makes the **long e** sound. Fill in the circle next to the word *no* if it does not make the **long e** sound. (2 points each.)

1. bumpy   Ⓐ yes Ⓑ no   3. dirty   Ⓐ yes Ⓑ no

2. fifty   Ⓐ yes Ⓑ no   4. happy   Ⓐ yes Ⓑ no

Integrated Activity

Using the weather section of a newspaper, cut out all of the **y** words where **y** makes the **long e** sound.

> Core Curriculum Concept: Identification of **y** words where **y** makes the **long e** vowel sound and use of those words in context.

Sounds of Y: long *i* sound (ī)

The sound of **y** at the end of words usually makes the **long i** sound if the word does not have other vowels in it. The word *try* is a good example.

Direct Activity

Below each picture write *yes* if the **y** sound at the end of the word makes the **long i** sound or *no* if it does not make the **long i** sound. (2 points each.)

1.

cry

y e s

2.

sticky

_____

3.

spy

_____

Writing Practice

Read the words below. If the **y** ending makes the **long i** sound, circle it. If the **y** ending does not make the **long i** sound put an X through it. Use each word in a sentence and put a rectangle around it. (2 points each.)

1. (pry)   We could not [pry] the crab off of his toe. _____

2. crazy   _____

          _____

3. sly   _____

          _____

Test-Taking Skills

Fill in the circle next to the word *yes* if the **y** ending makes the **long i** sound, fill in the circle next to the word *no* if it does not make the **long i** sound. (2 points each.)

1. frumpy   Ⓐ yes ●Ⓑ no   **3.** my   Ⓐ yes Ⓑ no

2. shy   Ⓐ yes Ⓑ no   **4.** slippery   Ⓐ yes Ⓑ no

Integrated Activity

Using one page of the newspaper and your favorite color of crayon or marker, circle all of the words with the **long i** sound for **y** endings.

> Core Curriculum Concept: Identification of **y** words where **y** makes the **long i** vowel sound and use of those words in context.

Sounds of Y: long *e* and *i* sounds

Direct Activity

Unscramble the **long e y-ending** and **long i y-ending** words below. Draw a picture that matches each word. (2 points each.)

1.

upypp

p̶u̶p̶p̶y̶

2.

lyf

— — —

3.

zlay

— — — —

Writing Practice

Write a word with a **long i** or **long e y-ending** on the lines below. Then write your own definition for the word you chose. (2 points each.)

1. **long i** p̶r̶y̶   to separate two objects that are stuck together by pulling them apart.

2. **long e** _____ _____

3. **long i** _____ _____

Test-Taking Skills

Fill in the circle next to the correct sound of **y** for each word below. (2 points each.)

1. milky Ⓐ long ē Ⓑ long ī Ⓒ neither   3. dry Ⓐ long ē Ⓑ long ī Ⓒ neither

2. clay Ⓐ long ē Ⓑ long ī Ⓒ neither   4. foamy Ⓐ long ē Ⓑ long ī Ⓒ neither

Integrated Activity

Make a "Word Link" picture with either **long e y-ending** words or **long i y-ending** words. Write a word in the center of a page; then think of another word that uses one of those letters and "link" the second word to the first with that letter. Make 10 links.

        Example: Long ē
                 Fluf fy
                      u
                      n
                 pu   ny
                      y

> Core Curriculum Concept: Identification of **y** words where **y** makes the **long e** vowel sound and use of those words in context.

43

Sounds of Y: long *e* and *i* sounds

Activity

For each number below, circle the words that have the **long e y-ending** and put an X on the words with **long i y-endings**. Then, in the dot to dot, draw a line from the first number with a circled word from the list to the next number with a circled word from the list. Skip the number dots that have been X'ed. (20 points.)

(When you are finished, fill in the word below the picture that tells what the picture is. Hint: the picture's name has a long *e y*-ending.)

___ ___ ___ ___ Y

1. (stormy)	6. my	11. crispy	16. why
2. ~~dry~~	7. try	12. story	17. pry
3. (crazy)	8. rainy	13. sly	18. sty
4. silly	9. sloppy	14. by	19. worry
5. happy	10. spy	15. jolly	20. frenzy

> **Core Curriculum Concept:** Identification and decoding of **y** words where **y** makes the **long i** and **long e** vowel sounds.

Hard and Soft C and G: hard *c* sound

When followed by the vowels **e, i,** or **y,** the sound of **c** is usually **soft**, as in the word *cement*. When followed by any other letter, or none at all, the **c** usually makes the **hard** sound, as in *cat* and *picnic*.

Direct Activity

Put a triangle around all of the **hard c** sounds in the words below. Put an X on the **soft c** sounds. (2 points each.)

1. Crispy   **2.** lace   **3.** camel

Writing Practice

Circle each of the words that have the **hard c** sound, and put an X on the words that have the **soft c** sound. Use each word in a sentence and circle it. (2 points each.)

1. octopus   An octopus lives in the ocean. _____

_____

2. cinema   _____

_____

3. camera   _____

_____

Test-Taking Skills

Fill in the circle next to the word with a **hard c** sound. (2 points each.)

1. Ⓐ clap
   Ⓑ rice
   Ⓒ cinnamon
   Ⓓ center

2. Ⓐ cent
   Ⓑ sauce
   Ⓒ crane
   Ⓓ dice

3. Ⓐ nice
   Ⓑ picture
   Ⓒ cell
   Ⓓ force

4. Ⓐ dice
   Ⓑ call
   Ⓒ centipede
   Ⓓ trace

Integrated Activity

Write down as many people's names as you can think of that have the letter c in them. Circle all of the **hard c** sounds and put rectangles around all of the **soft c** sounds.

> Core Curriculum Concept: Identification of the **hard sound of c**, as in the word *car*, and the **soft sound of c**, as in the word *ice*. Use of those words in context.

Hard and Soft C and G: soft *c* sound

Direct Activity

Put a rectangle around all of the **soft c** sounds in the words below. Put a line through all the **hard c** sounds. (2 points each.)

1.

c i r c l e

2.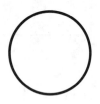

_ _ _ _ _

3.

_ _ _ _ _ _ _

Writing Practice

Circle each of the words that have the **soft c** sound and put an X on the words that have the **hard c** sound. Use each word in a sentence. (2 points each.)

1. (cellophane) We wrapped the Easter basket in colored plastic (cellophane) so it would look nice.

2. lacy _____

_____

3. cattle _____

_____

Test-Taking Skills

Fill in the circle next to the word with a **soft c** sound. (2 points each.)

1. Ⓐ pickle
   Ⓑ come
   ● place
   Ⓓ colt

2. Ⓐ crayon
   Ⓑ wince
   Ⓒ candle
   Ⓓ nickel

3. Ⓐ fraction
   Ⓑ actor
   Ⓒ quince
   Ⓓ cushion

4. Ⓐ cool
   Ⓑ dance
   Ⓒ microphone
   Ⓓ scare

Integrated Activity

Make "Cat's Cradle Words" by writing cursive **c** words with string on construction paper. After you've written three **soft c** words and three **hard c** words with the string, you can tie the ends together and play Cat's Cradle with a friend!

> Core Curriculum Concept: Identification of the **hard sound of c**, as in the word *car*, and the **soft sound of c**, as in the word *ice*. Use of those words in context.

Hard and Soft C and G: hard *g* sound

When followed by the vowels **e**, **i**, or **y**, the sound of **g** is usually **soft**, as in the word *age*. When followed by any other letter, or none at all, the **g** usually makes the **hard** sound, as in *gold* and *tag*.

Direct Activity

Put a triangle around all of the **hard g** sounds in the words below. Put an X on the **soft g** sounds. (2 points each.)

1. grass   2. gorge   3. grand

Writing Practice

Circle each of the words that have the **hard g** sound and put an X on the **soft g** sound. Use each word in a sentence and circle it. (2 points each.)

1. juggle   My mom taught us how to juggle. _____

2. gasoline _____

_____

3. giant _____

_____

Test-Taking Skills

Fill in the circle next to the word with the **hard g** sound. (2 points each.)

1. Ⓐ sage
    Ⓑ giraffe
    Ⓒ general
    ● grant

2. Ⓐ giggle
    Ⓑ page
    Ⓒ gentle
    Ⓓ giant

3. Ⓐ sludge
    Ⓑ wage
    Ⓒ gift
    Ⓓ gel

4. Ⓐ girl
    Ⓑ budge
    Ⓒ cringe
    Ⓓ rage

Integrated Activity

Word Checkers—Make a checkerboard. Write one **hard g** word on each of the red starting squares and one **soft g** word on each of the black starting squares. With a partner, play a game of checkers using homemade checker pieces. Read the word on the square you want to move to; then say "hard *g*" or "soft *g*" for each *g* word. You can only move if you're right about the word and the *g* sound it makes!

> Core Curriculum Concept: Identification of the **hard sound of g**, as in the word *tag*, and the **soft sound of g**, as in the word *age*, and use of those words in context.

Hard and Soft C and G: soft *g* sound

Direct Activity

Put a rectangle around all of the **soft g** sounds in the words below. Put a line through all of the **hard g** sounds. (2 points each.)

1. gorilla   2. garage   3. cringe

Writing Practice

Circle each of the words that have the **soft g** sound and put an X on the words with the **hard g** sound. Use each word in a sentence and put a rectangle around the word. (2 points each.)

1. wagon   The little red wagon was a gift from my grandma.

2. George _____

3. dragon _____

Test-Taking Skills

Fill in the circle next to the word with the **soft g** sound. (2 points each.)

1. Ⓐ great
    Ⓑ organ
    ● stage
    Ⓓ grapes

2. Ⓐ pig
    Ⓑ gentleman
    Ⓒ gum
    Ⓓ grocery

3. Ⓐ gross
    Ⓑ frog
    Ⓒ generous
    Ⓓ peg

4. Ⓐ storage
    Ⓑ lagoon
    Ⓒ program
    Ⓓ hog

Integrated Activity

Word Checkers—Make a checkerboard. Write one **hard g** word on each of the red starting squares and one **soft g** word on each of the black starting squares. With a partner, play a game of checkers using checker pieces, milk jug lids, or construction paper circles. Read the word on the square you want to move to; then say "hard *g*" or "soft *g*" for each *g* word. You can only move if you're right about the word and the *g* sound it makes.

> Core Curriculum Concept: Identification of the **hard sound** of **g**, as in the word *tag*, and the **soft sound of g**, as in the word *age*, and use of those words in context.

Hard and Soft C and G: review

Activity

For each number below, circle the words with the **soft c** and **g** sounds and put an X on the words with **hard c** and **g** sounds. Then, in the dot to dot, draw a line from the first number with a circled word from the list to the next number with a circled word from the list. Skip the number dots that have been X'ed. (20 points.)

(When you are finished, try to fill in the word below the picture that tells what the picture is. Hint: the picture's name has a soft c in it.)

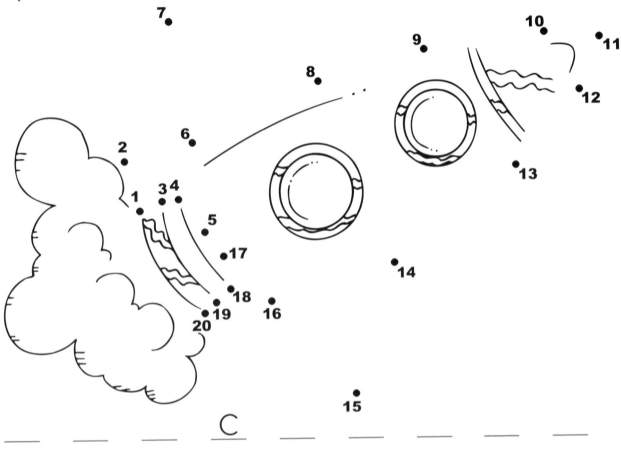

1. (face)   6. ice   11. nice   16. trace
2. octopus   7. nice   12. huge   17. clap
3. (strange)   8. stage   13. sage   18. cent
4. age   9. giant   14. giraffe   19. plunge
5. gas   10. city   15. celery   20. cinnamon

Core Curriculum Concept: Identification of the **hard** and **soft sound** of **c**, as in *cat* and *ice*, and the **hard** and **soft sound** of **g**, as in *tag* and *age*. Use of those words in context.

Hard and Soft C and G: review

Activity

Find at least twenty **c** and **g** words and circle them in the word search below. (There are over seventy words in all.)

```
m i c r o p h o n e l c a l l t r a c e u n e s s
y l i g k z d r a g o n g e n e r o u s h o g m j
n a o p i a i l p a g e f y s n i c e q y y a y n
l r i g l d l p u i e m q d c a m e r a j a w j r
n q c p e a z e d t n a i g e c c g c j j r h u o
o x e a f g c g c s a l l i r o g c u i f c i g c
m w n h n k o e e e r e w j a c y y w n x l g q
a x i l r d p q m p f d g e g a t s j a n c f l i
n f l z m d l h e a v v a i v l l b z g e w i e a
n e o g i n g e n r o g l n p l a y i o c b j p u
i t s c r a n e t g g p y r c l u r l n i i c f c
c c a g v r l t j o e m p t r e t n e c r e n k o
g d g o h g o u l g n e k b i x t e y n n h g c l
r g l r q y o d a g o l z p t c e c k t e r l h t
o g a f y q c r i p c c l a a c l i i j o g e x e
c r c b z a o g o m e r l l e e a p c s s o l s g
e a y n q t g u a w l i e c r y e m s o r q t b r
r n g z s l q r c u l c r w g d t d e g m q n k o
y t d r e j g e f f a r i g e i m r a l n e e r g
x h n z k o d w x f e q e p h z o n s d t w g b n
w e o h r x f t n e c c w g e t a g s i g t o y e
z g o p p d o g i f t r u d a s m m a c m q a l i
u a g h m s r g n u t a h a s r k u r e p z k c c
m s a h q p c f b u d g e t s k a g g q w e o d m
d c l r v e e n b j w e i u h h r g e t m g l b b
```

Write the words you find on the lines below. (20 points.)

_____   _____   _____

_____   _____   _____

_____   _____   _____

_____   _____   _____

_____   _____   _____

_____   _____   _____

Core Curriculum Concept: Identification of the **soft sound** of **c**, as in the words *cat* and *ice*, the **hard** and **soft sound of g**, as in the words *tag* and *age*. Use of those words in context.

Silent Consonants: *kn, wr,* and *sc*

Some consonants, when found together in a word, make one sound. When the letters **kn** are found together, the **k** is usually silent and we hear the **n** sound, as in the word *knot*. When the letters **wr** are found together, the **w** is silent but we hear the **r**, as in the word *wrong*. When the letters **sc** are found together, the **c** is often silent and we hear the **s** sound, as in *science*.

Direct Activity

Write the correct consonants—**kn**, **wr**, and **sc**—to finish the words below. (2 points each.)

1.

k n ee

2.

_ _ite

3.

_ _issors

Writing Practice

Circle the **silent consonants**. Then, use the word in a sentence and circle the word.
(2 points each.)

1. scent   In the spring the (scent) of blooming lilacs fills the air. _____

2. knock   _____
             _____

3. wrench   _____
             _____

Test-Taking Skills

Fill in the circle next to the consonants that correctly complete the word. (2 points each.)

1. _ _ong   Ⓐ wr   2. _ _ene   Ⓐ wr   3. _ _eel   Ⓐ wr   4. _ _ob   Ⓐ wr
            Ⓑ sc   Ⓑ sc   Ⓑ sc   Ⓑ sc
            Ⓒ kn   Ⓒ kn   Ⓒ kn   Ⓒ kn

Integrated Activity

Write as many words with **silent consonants** as you can in white crayon on a white piece of paper. Have a friend do the same. Then, trade papers and paint over the page with watercolors to reveal the words. Which words were the same and which ones were different?

> Core Curriculum Concept: Identification of silent consonants:
> *k* in **kn**, *w* in **wr**, and *c* in **sc**, sound-symbol association, and
> use of those words in context.

Silent Consonants: *kn, wr,* and *sc*

Direct Activity

Draw a line to connect the picture with the correct **consonants** in its name. (2 points each.)

1.

wr   sc   kn

2.

wr   sc   kn

3.

wr   sc   kn

Writing Practice

Choose a word with silent consonants **wr**, **sc,** or **kn** for a title. Then write a five-line rhyming poem about the word. (6 points.)

Science

Science is amazing,

It is so many things.

Bugs, birds, cars and people

Planes and kites with strings.

And even bells that ring!

_____

_____

_____

_____

_____

_____

Test-Taking Skills

Fill in the circle next to the correct **silent consonant** word that completes each sentence. (2 points each.)

1. When I laugh my nose _____ up.
   Ⓐ wrinkles   Ⓑ scents   Ⓒ knots   Ⓓ none of these

2. First I have to cut the paper with _____.
   Ⓐ kneads   Ⓑ wrecks   Ⓒ scissors   Ⓓ none of these

3. My brother has fixed our go-cart after two _____.
   Ⓐ knives   Ⓑ scientists   Ⓒ wrecks   Ⓓ none of these

4. My mother _____ the bread dough twice before it bakes.
   Ⓐ wriggles   Ⓑ kneads   Ⓒ scenes   Ⓓ none of these

Integrated Activity

Make up tongue twisters using as many words with silent consonants in them as you can.
Example: Wanda wraps her wrinkles in wallpaper.

> Core Curriculum Concept: Identification of silent consonants:
> *k* in **kn**, *w* in **wr** and *c* in **sc**, sound-symbol association, and
> use of those words in context.

Silent Consonants: *mb, ck,* and *gh*

Silent consonants can also be found at the end or in the middle of words. When the letters **mb** are found together, the **b** is usually silent and we hear the **m** sound, as in the word *lamb*. When the letters **ck** are found together, the **c** is silent and we hear the **k**, as in the word *stick*. And when the letters **gh** are found together, in some words they are both silent, as in the word *high*.

Direct Activity

Write the correct silent consonants—**mb**, **ck** or **gh**—to complete the words below. (2 points each.)

1.
ni g h t

2.
la_ _

3.
tri_ _

Writing Practice

Circle the **silent consonants**. Then use the word in a sentence and circle the word. (2 points each.)

1. co m(b)   After a shower I always (comb) my hair. _____

2. thick   _____

3. eight   _____

Test-Taking Skills

Fill in the circle next to the letters that correctly complete the word. (2 points each.)

1. li_ _t   ● gh
            Ⓑ mb
            Ⓒ ck

2. si_ _   Ⓐ ck
            Ⓑ gh
            Ⓒ A&B

3. thu_ _   Ⓐ gh
            Ⓑ ck
            Ⓒ mb

4. fi_ _t   Ⓐ mb
            Ⓑ gh
            Ⓒ ck

Integrated Activity

Write one silent consonant word in big letters on a piece of paper. Then draw a picture that goes with the word. Make the letters part of the picture!

Core Curriculum Concept: Identification of silent consonants: *b* in **mb**, *c* in **ck** and **gh**, sound-symbol association, and use of those words in context.

Silent Consonants: *mb, ck,* and *gh*

Direct Activity

Draw a line to connect the picture with the correct **consonants** in its name. (2 points each.)

1.   2.   3.

gh   ck   mb   gh   ck   mb   gh   sc   mb

Writing Practice

Choose a word with silent consonants **mb**, **ck**, or **gh** as a title. Then write a five-line poem about that word. (6 points.)

Might
A knight may fight
For what is right
But to use his might
He can't lose sight
Of wrong and right.

Test-Taking Skills

Fill in the circle next to the correct **silent consonant** word that completes each sentence. (2 points each.)

1. I really like to _____ sparklers on the 4th of July.
   Ⓐ comb   ⬤ light   Ⓒ kick   Ⓓ none of these
2. The hammer missed and hit my _____.
   Ⓐ thumb   Ⓑ tight   Ⓒ sick   Ⓓ none of these
3. The cookie was so good I ate every _____.
   Ⓐ crack   Ⓑ sight   Ⓒ crumb   Ⓓ none of these
4. We put a _____ in each poster to hang them on the wall.
   Ⓐ sigh   Ⓑ tomb   Ⓒ tack   Ⓓ none of these

Integrated Activity

Write down several **silent consonant** words on strips of paper. Put them in a bowl or bag. Choose three words and use them to make a silly sentence. Put them back into the bowl and keep making silly sentences with the words you choose until you run out of silly sentences.

Core Curriculum Concept: Identification of silent consonants: *b* in **mb**, *c* in **ck** and **gh**, sound-symbol association, and use of those words in context.

Endings: *ed*

Adding **ed** shows that an action word has taken place already. For example, "**Mail** this letter, please." and "I **mailed** it this morning."

When one word ends with one vowel followed by one consonant, the ending consonant is doubled before adding **ed**. For example, **wag + ed = wagged**.

Direct Activity

Rewrite each word below adding an **ed** ending. (2 points each.)

1. step   stepped
2. hand   _____
3. hug   _____

Writing Practice

Choose a word for each number from the list below. Add an **ed** ending. Use that word in a sentence and circle it. Put a line through the word you chose from the list below. (2 points each.)

stop   play   clap   wish   ~~sculpt~~   pat

1. sculpt +ed = sculpted   She (sculpted) a flower out of clay.
2. _____ +ed = _____   _____
3. _____ +ed = _____   _____

Test-Taking Skills

Fill in the circle next to the word with the correct **ed** ending. (2 points each.)

1. point + ed = Ⓐ pointted   ● pointed   © poinnted
2. stay + ed   = Ⓐ stayyed   Ⓑ stayed   © stayd
3. trust + ed = Ⓐ trusted   Ⓑ trustted   © trussted

Integrated Activity

Choose a recipe from a recipe book. Write down all of the action words (like stir, cook, boil, etc.) on a piece of paper. Add **ed** endings to each word and rewrite the recipe by replacing the action words with the *ed* ending words. For example, "Stir the sugar water," would become "Stirred the sugar water."

> Core Curriculum Concept: Identifying words containing **ed** endings and adding **ed** to verbs in isolation and in context.

Endings: *y* + *ed*

When adding **ed** to words ending with a consonant **y** change the **y** to **i** and add **ed**. For example, marr**y** **+ ed** = marr**ied**.

Direct Activity

Rewrite each word below by adding an **ed** ending. (2 points each.)

1. carry   _carried_

2. fry   _____

3. scurry   _____

Writing Practice

Choose a word for each number from the list below. Add an **ed** ending, use that word in a sentence, and circle it. Put a line through the word you chose from the list below. (2 points each.)

try   copy   worry   pry   cry   study

1. _try_ + ed = _tried_   I (tried) my best on the spelling test.

2. _____ + ed = _____   _____

3. _____ + ed = _____   _____

Test-Taking Skills

Fill in the circle next to the word with the correct **ed** ending. (2 points each.)

1. worry + ed =   Ⓐ worred   Ⓑ worryed   🅲 worried

2. hurry + ed =   Ⓐ hurried   Ⓑ hurryed   Ⓒ hurryd

3. party + ed =   Ⓐ partyed   Ⓑ partied   Ⓒ partyd

4. bury + ed =   Ⓐ buryed   Ⓑ buried   Ⓒ buryd

Integrated Activity

Matching Game—Write the **y-ending** words from this page on index cards (one word per card); then change the **y** to **i** and add **ed** for each word and write the new words on index cards. Turn them face down on a table and try to pair the words with their *ed* ending match by turning over two cards at a time. If they do not match, turn them face down and try again. (You can play on your own or with a partner.)

> Core Curriculum Concept: Identifying words containing **y** + **ed** endings and adding **ed** to verbs with **y** endings in isolation and in context.

Endings: *e + ed*

When adding **ed** to words ending in silent **e,** drop the **e** and add **ed**. For example, wav**e +
ed** = wav**ed**.

Direct Activity

Rewrite each word below by adding an **ed** ending. (2 points each.)

1. love   ~~loved~~
2. slice   _____
3. bake   _____

Writing Practice

Choose a word for each number from the list below. Add an **ed** ending, use that word in a
sentence, and put a triangle around it. Put a line through the word you chose from the list
below. (2 points each.)

bike save hike race like ~~force~~

1. force   +ed = forced   I forced the air out of the balloon.
2. _____ +ed = _____   _____
3. _____ +ed = _____   _____

Test-Taking Skills

Fill in the circle next to the word with the correct **ed** ending. (2 points each.)

1. move + ed =   Ⓐ moveed   Ⓑ movd   ⬤ moved
2. place + ed = Ⓐ placd   Ⓑ placed   © placeed
3. pile + ed = Ⓐ pileed   Ⓑ pild   © piled
4. phone + ed = Ⓐ phoned   Ⓑ phoneed   © phond

Integrated Activity

Write the **silent e-ending** words from this page on index cards, adding **ed** to each word
(one *ed* word per card). Think of other silent *e*-ending words that you can add *ed* to and
write those *ed* words on index cards. Put the cards in a pile with the words face down. With
a partner, take turns choosing a word and drawing a picture clue on paper. See if the other
person can guess the word from the picture clues you drew. You may use the *ed* words from
this page and the page before if you need help.

> Core Curriculum Concept: Identifying words containing **e +
> ed** endings and adding **e + ed** to verbs with **e** endings in
> isolation and in context.

www.summerbridgeactivities.com   Phonics—Grade 3—RBP0253

Endings: *ing*

Adding **ing** shows that an action is happening. For example, "**Mail** this letter, please," "I am **mailing** it." Also, "Watch the bird **fly**." and "The bird is **flying** south."

When a word ends with one vowel followed by one consonant the ending consonant is doubled before adding *ing*. For example, wa**g** + **ing** =wa**gging**.

Direct Activity

Rewrite each word below by adding an **ing** ending. (2 points each.)

1. hem   hemming
2. twist   _____
3. tap   _____

Tappity, Tappity, Tap

Writing Practice

Choose a word for each number from the list below. Add an **ing** ending. Use that word in a sentence and put a rectangle around it. Put a line through the word you chose from the list below. (2 points each.)

sit   wrap   stand   try   skip   ~~hiss~~

1. hiss   + ing = hissing   The snakes at the zoo were hissing.
2. _____ + ing = _____ _____
3. _____ + ing = _____ _____

Test-Taking Skills

Fill in the circle next to the word with the correct **ing** ending. (2 points each.)

1. cry + ing = Ⓐ crying   Ⓑ cring   © cryeing
2. find + ing = Ⓐ findding   Ⓑ findeing   © finding
3. wag + ing = Ⓐ wagging   Ⓑ waging   © wageing
4. dry + ing = Ⓐ dryeing   Ⓑ dring   © drying

Integrated Activity

Play tic-tac-toe with **ing** words. Choose two *ing* ending words, like *circling* and *crossing*. Use the words in place of X's and O's. (You can play by yourself or with a partner.)

Core Curriculum Concept: Identifying words containing **ing** endings and adding **ing** to verbs in isolation and in context.

Endings: *e* + *ing*

When adding **ing** to words ending in **silent e**, drop the **e** and add **ing**. For example, the word wav**e** + **ing** = **waving**.

Direct Activity

Rewrite each word below by adding an **ing** ending. (2 points each.)

1. chase _chasing_
2. skate _____
3. drive _____

Writing Practice

Choose a word for each number from the list below. Add an **ing** ending. Use that word in a sentence and circle it. Put a line through the word you chose from the list below. (2 points each.)

trace ~~waste~~ hope tape wipe race

1. _waste_ + ing = _wasting_   He was (wasting) too much paper.
2. _____ + ing = _____ _____
3. _____ + ing = _____ _____

Test-Taking Skills

Fill in the circle next to the word with the correct **ing** ending. (2 points each.)

1. raise + ing = Ⓐ raissing   ● raising   © raiseing
2. taste + ing = Ⓐ tasting   Ⓑ tasteing   © tastting
3. staple + ing = Ⓐ staplling   Ⓑ stapling   © stapeling
4. erase + ing = Ⓐ eraseing   Ⓑ erassing   © erasing

Integrated Activity

Write down all of the **silent e-ending** words from this page on strips of paper. Fold them and put them into a bowl or a bag. Choose a word and spell it, out loud, with the **ing** ending. Keep choosing words until all of them have been correctly spelled with the *ing* ending.

Core Curriculum Concept: Identifying **e**-ending words containing **ing** endings and adding **ing** to verbs with **e**-endings in isolation and in context.

www.summerbridgeactivities.com   Phonics—Grade 3—RBP0253

Endings: *ing* and *ed*

Direct Activity

Rewrite each word below adding the correct ending. (2 points each.)

1. tag + ing = _tagging_
2. stake + ed = _____
3. spy + ed = _____

Writing Practice

Choose a word for each number from the list below. Add an **ing** or **ed** ending. Use that word in a sentence and put a triangle around it. Put a line through the word you chose from the list below. (2 points each.)

wad   scare   ~~apply~~   wash   share   marry

1. _apply_ + ed = _applied_   My sister △applied△ for a nursing job.
2. _____ + ing = _____
3. _____ + ing = _____

Test-Taking Skills

Fill in the circle next to the word with the correct **ing** or **ed** ending. (2 points each.)

1. mark + ed   = Ⓐ markking   Ⓑ markeing   ● marked
2. rhyme + ing = Ⓐ rhyming   Ⓑ rhymeing   Ⓒ rhymming
3. jog + ed   = Ⓐ joged   Ⓑ jogd   Ⓒ jogged
4. dry + ed   = Ⓐ dryed   Ⓑ dried   Ⓒ dryd

Integrated Activity

I Spy, I Spied—Write down all the words from this page with their **ed** and **ing** endings on strips of paper. Count them and hide them around the room. Now, see if you can find each word and say a sentence, out loud, with that word in it.

Core Curriculum Concept: Identifying words containing **ed** and **ing** endings and adding **ed** and **ing** to verbs in isolation and in context; identifying **y-ending** words and adding **ed** and **ing** to **y-ending** verbs in isolation and in context.

Phonics—Grade 3—RBP0253   www.summerbridgeactivities.com   ©RBP Books

Endings: *s* and *y* + *s* = *ies*

The letter **s** can be added to some action words to form new words, like **walk + s = walks**. When an action word ends in **y**, change the **y** to **i** and add **es**. For example, **hurry + s = hurries**.

Direct Activity

Rewrite each action word below adding an **s ending**. (2 points each.)

1. marry   ~~marries~~
2. study   _____
3. cook   _____

Writing Practice

Choose a word for each number from the list below. Add an **s ending**. Use that word in a sentence and put a rectangle around it. Put a line through the word you chose from the list below. (2 points each.)

talk   carry   ~~dance~~   fry   sing   copy

1. dance   +s =   dances   Zoe dances in her tutu.
2. _____ +s =   _____   _____
3. _____ +s =   _____   _____

Test-Taking Skills

Fill in the circle next to the word with the correct **s ending**. (2 points each.)

1. stand + s   =   Ⓐ standes   ● stands   Ⓒ standies
2. worry + s   =   Ⓐ worrys   Ⓑ worries   Ⓒ worryes
3. help + s   =   Ⓐ helps   Ⓑ helpes   Ⓒ helpies
4. hurry + s   =   Ⓐ hurryes   Ⓑ hurrys   Ⓒ hurries

Integrated Activity

Write down the **s ending** words on this page on strips of paper. Glue them onto a sheet of your favorite color of construction paper. Separate the *ies* endings from the other *s* endings.

Core Curriculum Concept: Identifying verbs containing **s endings** and adding **s** to verbs in isolation and in context; identifying **y-ending** verbs containing **s endings** and adding **s** to **y-ending** verbs in isolation and in context.

Endings: *es*

The letters **es** are added to verbs ending in **s**, **ss**, **sh**, **ch**, or **x** to form new words, like the words ca**tch** and cat**ches**.

Direct Activity

Rewrite each verb below adding an **es** ending. (2 points each.)

1. cash _____cashes_____
2. bus _____
3. brush _____

Writing Practice

Add an **es** ending to the words below. Use at least six words in a silly story and put a triangle around the words you use. Put a line through the word you chose from the list below. (6 points.)

pitch__es   push__   box__
mix__   miss__   watch__
hiss__   wish__es   fax__

The boy pitches three outs and wishes he was... _____

_____

_____

Test-Taking Skills

Fill in the circle beside an **es** ending word that makes sense in each sentence. (2 points each.)

1. Marty _____ his muscles.
   Ⓐ flexes   Ⓑ crunches   Ⓒ shows
2. Alice _____ the cookies she baked around the room.
   Ⓐ mixes   Ⓑ sends   Ⓒ passes
3. My little sister _____ up in my mom's clothes.
   Ⓐ dresses   Ⓑ fixes   Ⓒ sneaks
4. The government _____ the people to help fund many programs.
   Ⓐ faxes   Ⓑ taxes   Ⓒ asks

Integrated Activity

Word Switches—Choose an **es** ending word from this page and write it down. Go through the alphabet and put each letter, one at a time, in place of the first letter in that word. Write down each new word you make. Circle all of the words that are real words and put an X on the others. For example: fixes = a. aixes, b. bixes, c. cixes, etc. How many real words did you make?

> Core Curriculum Concept: Identifying verbs containing **es** endings and adding **es** to verbs in isolation and in context that end in **s**, **ss**, **sh**, **ch** or **x**.

Base Words and Endings

Any word that can have an ending added to it is a **base word**. For example, **run** is the base word in **running**.

Direct Activity

Write the **base word** for the words below. (2 points each.)

1. pitches   pitch _____
2. singing   _____
3. fished   _____

Writing Practice

Add a **base word** from the list to the numbered items below. Add the ending indicated and use it in a new sentence. Circle the new words in each. Put a line through the word you chose from the list below. (2 points each.)

hug   close   stand   dry   ~~wash~~   make

1. wash   + es =   washes   Mom (washes) dishes while I dry them.
2. _____ + ing = _____   _____
3. _____ + ed = _____   _____

Test-Taking Skills

Fill in the circle next to the **base word** of the underlined word in each sentence. (2 points each.)

1. The girl <u>rides</u> her horse every day.
   - Ⓐ ride
   - Ⓑ rid
   - Ⓒ ridd
   - Ⓓ none of these
2. I enjoy <u>tapping</u> to the music!
   - Ⓐ tapp
   - Ⓑ tape
   - Ⓒ tap
   - Ⓓ none of these
3. The brown dog <u>catches</u> the Frisbee while jumping in the air.
   - Ⓐ cat
   - Ⓑ catche
   - Ⓒ catch
   - Ⓓ none of these
4. Aunt Jill <u>framed</u> the picture I drew for her.
   - Ⓐ frame
   - Ⓑ fram
   - Ⓒ framm
   - Ⓓ none of these

Integrated Activity

With a pen, crayon, or marker, highlight (or underline) all of the **base words** you can find on a page from your local newspaper.

> Core Curriculum Concept: Identifying base words and endings in isolation and in context; adding endings to base words and using them in context.

Endings: *ed*, *ing*, *s*, and *es*

Activity

Find your way through the maze by connecting words with correct endings and base words. Put an X through words that are not correct, and circle the correct words. (20 points.)

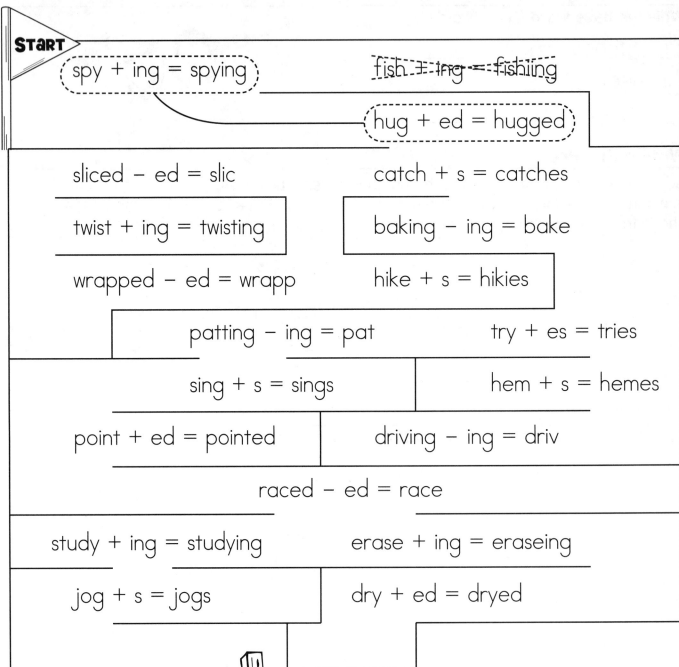

START

spy + ing = spying

~~fish + ing = fishing~~

hug + ed = hugged

sliced – ed = slic

catch + s = catches

twist + ing = twisting

baking – ing = bake

wrapped – ed = wrapp

hike + s = hikies

patting – ing = pat

try + es = tries

sing + s = sings

hem + s = hemes

point + ed = pointed

driving – ing = driv

raced – ed = race

study + ing = studying

erase + ing = eraseing

jog + s = jogs

dry + ed = dryed

FINISH

Core Curriculum Concept: Identification of words containing **ed** endings, **ing** endings, **s** endings, and **es** endings, and identification of base words.

Endings: *er*

The ending **er** is placed at the end of words to show "more." For example, the word **great + er = greater**, which means **more great**. (The ending **er** shows a comparison between two things.)

Direct Activity

Rewrite each word adding **er** to the end. Draw a picture to show the word's new meaning. (2 points each.)

1. tight ___tighter___
2. cheap _____
3. thick _____

1.	2.	3.

Writing Practice

Choose a word from the list below and add **er** to the end. Then, write a sentence using that word. Circle the er words in each sentence. Put a line through the word you chose from the list below. (2 points each.)

long sick poor rich neat fast

1. _sick_ + er = _sicker_   My stomach is feeling much (sicker.)
2. _____ + er = _____   _____
3. _____ + er = _____   _____

Test-Taking Skills

Fill in the circle next to the correct meaning of each **er** word. (2 points each.)

1. brighter   Ⓐ more right   ● more bright   Ⓒ not as bright
2. smaller   Ⓐ more all   Ⓑ more small   Ⓒ not as small
3. lighter   Ⓐ not as light   Ⓑ more little   Ⓒ more light
4. slower   Ⓐ more slow   Ⓑ not as slow   Ⓒ less slow

Integrated Activity

Shape pieces of aluminum foil into as many **er** words as you can. For example, crumple a piece of foil into a ball to show the word **small**; then crumple up a tighter ball to show the word **smaller**.

> Core Curriculum Concept: Identifying words containing **er** endings and the meaning of those words; adding **er** to words in isolation, and using those words in context.

www.summerbridgeactivities.com   Phonics—Grade 3—RBP0253

Endings: *est*

The ending **est** is placed at the end of words to show "most." For example, the word **great + est = greatest** meaning **most great**. (The ending **er** usually shows a comparison between two things, while **est** shows a comparison between three or more things.)

Direct Activity

Rewrite each word adding **est** to the end. Draw pictures to show the word's new meaning. (2 points each.)

1. mean meaner <u>meanest</u>
2. young younger _____
3. tall   taller   _____

1.	2.	3.

Writing Practice

Choose a base word from the list below. Add **est** to show the most. Then, write a sentence using that word and circle the *est* words in each sentence. Put a line through the base word you chose from the list below. (2 points each.)

~~quiet~~   cold   warm   weak   sweet   wild

1. <u>quiet</u> + est = <u>quietest</u>   I think turtles are the (quietest) animals.
2. _____ + est = _____   _____
3. _____ + est = _____   _____

Test-Taking Skills

Fill in the circle next to the correct meaning of each **est** word. (2 points each.)

1. smallest Ⓐ more small Ⓑ not as small ● most small
2. fastest   Ⓐ most fast   Ⓑ more fast   Ⓒ not as fast
3. shortest Ⓐ not as short Ⓑ more short Ⓒ most short
4. strongest Ⓐ most strong Ⓑ not as strong Ⓒ more strong

Integrated Activity

The Longest Chain—Write all the **est** words you know on strips of colored paper. Glue them together to make a chain and see how far it will go around the room!

> Core Curriculum Concept: Identifying words containing **est** endings and the meaning of those words; adding **est** to words in isolation and using those words in context.

Endings: *y + er* and *y = est*

When words end in **y** change the **y** to **i** before adding **er** or **est**. For example, the word **busy + er** becomes **busier**, and **busy + est** becomes **busiest**.

Direct Activity

Add the correct **er** or **est** ending to each **y** word. Draw a picture to show the word's new meaning. (2 points each.)

1. happy   <u>happier</u>   <u>happiest</u>
2. lovely   _____   _____
3. bubbly   _____   _____

1.	2.	3.

Writing Practice

Complete the ads below by using words that end in **y + er** and **y + est** to describe the products. Put a rectangle around the er words and a circle around the *est* words. You may use words from this page if you need help. (2 points each.)

Sudsy soap is __sudsier__ (er) than other soaps. It's the _____ (est) and _____ (er) soap for your bath!

Crispy Crunch Cereal is _____ (er) and _____ (er) than other cereals. It's the _____ (est) cereal at your breakfast table!

Test-Taking Skills

Fill in the circle next to the word with the correct **est** or **er** ending. (2 points each.)

1. silly + er   = Ⓐ sillyer   Ⓑ siller   ⬤ sillier
2. pretty + est = Ⓐ prettiest   Ⓑ prettyest   Ⓒ prettest
3. crazy + er = Ⓐ crazyer   Ⓑ crazier   Ⓒ crazer
4. messy + est = Ⓐ messyest   Ⓑ messiest   Ⓒ messest

Integrated Activity

Choose an item in the room and write a commercial to sell it using as many **y + er** and **y + est** words as you can think of. Draw pictures of your commercial being shown on TV!

> Core Curriculum Concept: Identifying words containing **y + er** and **y + est** endings and the meaning of those words; adding **er** and **est** to **y-ending** words in isolation and using those words in context.

Name _____   Date _____

Endings: vowel-consonant endings + *er* and *est*

When words end with one vowel followed by one consonant, like the Word *big*, double the consonant and then add **er** or **est**. For example, the word **big + er = bigger** and **big + est = biggest**.

Direct Activity

Add **er** and **est** to each word. Draw a picture to show the word's new meaning. (2 points each.)

1. thin ___thinner___ ___thinnest___
2. wet _____ _____
3. fat _____ _____

1. 	2.	3.

Writing Practice

Add **er** or **est** to the vowel consonant words below. Use each one in a sentence. Circle the *er* and *est* words. (2 points each.)

1. big_____ + est= ___biggest___ I saw the (biggest) cookie in the world!
2. red_____ + er = _____ _____
3. hot_____ + est= _____ _____

Test-Taking Skills

Fill in the circle next to the **double-consonant word** that best completes the sentence. (2 points each.)

1. In the play the scientist is _____ than the monster.
   Ⓐ crazier   ● madder   Ⓒ sicker
2. The pit bull is the _____ dog of all.
   Ⓐ ugliest   Ⓑ meanest   Ⓒ none of these
3. The movie "Old Yeller" is the _____ show I've ever seen.
   Ⓐ saddest   Ⓑ angriest   Ⓒ slowest
4. I think the table is _____ than the ground.
   Ⓐ plainer   Ⓑ yuckier   Ⓒ flatter

Integrated Activity

Draw a large oval racetrack on a piece of paper. Push paper clips in a race with a partner around the track. Take turns being the commentator and use **er** and **est** words to tell about the race and who is winning. Example: "Tom is getting off to a **slower** start than Jim, but his car is **speedier** around the corners…"

Core Curriculum Concept: Identifying vowel-consonant words containing **er** and **est** endings and the meaning of those words; adding **er** and **est** to vowel-consonant words in isolation and using those words in context.

Name _____   Date _____

Endings: silent *e* endings + *er* and *est*

When a word has a **silent e**-ending like *cute*, drop the **e** before adding **er** or **est**. For example, **cute + er** becomes **cuter,** and **cute + est** becomes **cutest**.

Direct Activity

Write the **base word** for each number before er and est were added. Draw a picture to match. (2 points each.)

1. _cute_   cuter   cutest
2. _____   nicer   nicest
3. _____   wiser   wisest

1.
2.
3.

Writing Practice

Add **er** or **est** to the **silent e**-endings below. Use them in a sentence. Circle the *er* words and put a rectangle around the est words. (2 points each.)

1. blue   + er = _bluer_   The sky was (bluer) today than yesterday.
2. white   + est= _____   _____
3. little   + er = _____   _____

Test-Taking Skills

Fill in the circle next to the **silent e**-ending word **+ er** or **est** that best completes the sentence. Remember that *er* shows a comparison between two things, and *est* shows a comparison between three or more things. (2 points each.)

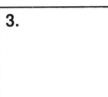

1. That color is the _____ purple I've ever seen!
   Ⓐ truest   Ⓑ truer   Ⓒ truly
2. This baking soda is _____ than salt.
   Ⓐ fine   Ⓑ finest   Ⓒ finer
3. The swamp monster is _____ than Frankenstein.
   Ⓐ vile   Ⓑ viler   Ⓒ vilest
4. This book is the _____ of all three.
   Ⓐ rare   Ⓑ rarer   Ⓒ rarest

Integrated Activity

Across the top of a piece of paper write down the words for three things you see in the room. For example, chair, book, table. Use **er** and **est** words to compare those three things. Write the *er* or *est* word below the thing it describes.

For example:

chair	book	table
taller than the book	smallest	tallest etc.

Core Curriculum Concept: Identifying **silent** e-ending words containing **er** and **est** endings and the meaning of those words; adding **er** and **est** to **silent** e-ending words in isolation and using those words in context.

www.summerbridgeactivities.com   Phonics—Grade 3—RBP0253

Endings: *er* and *est*

Activity

To discover the phrase below, put an X over the incorrect *er* and *est* words and circle the correct *er* and *est* words for each number. Then, fill in each space with the underlined letter of the circled (or correct) *er* and *est* words in order. (The first two are done for you.) (20 points.)

Y O _ ' _ _ _   _ _ _

_ _ _ _ _ _ _ _!

1. yummy + er = <u>y</u>ummier
2. cold + est = <u>c</u>oldest
3. ugly + er = <u>u</u>glier
4. red + est = <u>r</u>eddest
5. early + est = <u>e</u>arliest
6. young + er = you<u>n</u>gger
7. tiny + est = <u>t</u>iniest
8. fast + est = <u>f</u>astiest
9. hard + er = <u>h</u>arder
10. new + er = n<u>e</u>wer
11. pretty + er = p<u>r</u>etter
12. big + est = bi<u>g</u>gest
13. true + er = t<u>r</u>uer
14. healthy + er = h<u>e</u>althier
15. wet + est = <u>w</u>etest
16. small + est = sm<u>a</u>llest
17. tight + est = tigh<u>t</u>est
18. messy + er = m<u>e</u>ssier
19. wise + er = wi<u>s</u>er
20. quiet + est = quie<u>t</u>est

Core Curriculum Concept: Identification of words containing **er** and **est** endings.

Phonics—Grade 3—RBP0253
www.summerbridgeactivities.com
©RBP Books

Plurals: adding *s*

A **singular** word is a word that stands for one of something. To make most singular words **plural**, simply **add** an **s** to the end. For example, **hat + s** becomes **hats**.

Direct Activity

Add an **s** to the words below to make them plural. Rewrite the word; then draw a picture to match the new word. (2 points each.)

1. toy   _toys_____

2. can   _____

3. pile   _____

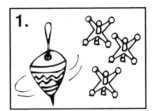

1.	2.	3.

Writing Practice

Make a grocery list for Mom by adding **s** to words making them plural. (2 points each.)

We need to buy _grapes_(grape), _____(pear), _____(pickle), _____(egg), _____(apple), _____(roll), and _____(orange) at the store.

Test-Taking Skills

Fill in the circle next to the **plural** word that best fits each clue. (2 points each.)

1. Things that make a job easier   Ⓐ tools   Ⓑ jewels   Ⓒ rings

2. Things you can wear   Ⓐ swings   Ⓑ bikes   Ⓒ skates

3. Items you clean with   Ⓐ pens   Ⓑ crayons   Ⓒ brooms

4. Things you would eat off   Ⓐ chairs   Ⓑ tables   Ⓒ stools

Integrated Activity

Using magazine and newspaper ads cut out pictures of some candies that have a **plural** name and glue them on paper. Write the plural name of each candy below its picture.

Core Curriculum Concept: Identifying plurals in isolation and their meaning, and using plurals in context; adding **s**.

71

Plurals: *es*

When a singular word ends in **ch**, **sh**, **s**, **ss**, or **x**, add an **es** to make it plural. For example, **fox + es** becomes **foxes**.

Direct Activity

Add an **es** to the words below to make them plural. Write it down; then draw a picture to match the new word. (2 points each.)

1. dish   _dishes_
2. branch _____
3. kiss   _____

1.	2.	3.

Writing Practice

Complete Mom's "To Do List" by adding **es** to the words in parentheses. (2 points each.)

The things I have to do: make _lunches_ (lunch), wash _____(dish), plant_____(grass), ride the _____(bus), feed the _____(finch), wind the _____(watch) and send the _____(fax).

Test-Taking Skills

Fill in the circle next to the plural **es** word that best fits each clue. (2 points each.)

1. These are put into material with a needle and thread.
   - Ⓐ stitches   Ⓑ mosses   Ⓒ lashes
2. A genie in a bottle may grant you three of these.
   - Ⓐ wishes   Ⓑ taxes   Ⓒ losses
3. You might pack things into these.
   - Ⓐ crutches   Ⓑ messes   Ⓒ boxes
4. These are tools used to chop wood.
   - Ⓐ benches   Ⓑ axes   Ⓒ branches

Integrated Activity

Put a squiggly line around all the plural **es** words you can find on a newspaper page. How many were there?

> Core Curriculum Concept: Identifying plurals in isolation and their meaning, and using plurals in context; adding **es**.

Plurals: *y* + *s* = *ies*

When a singular word ends in *y*, change the **y** to **i** and add **es** to make it plural. For example, the word **candy + es = candies**.

Direct Activity

Change the singular words below to plural words. Circle the **singular** and **plural endings**.
(2 points each.)

1. pans(y)   pans(ies)
2. story   _____
3. bunny   _____

Writing Practice

Rewrite four of the *y*-ending words below with **plural** endings. Then write sentences using two of the plural words in each sentence. Put a line through the words you use.
(2 points each.)

~~family~~ ~~history~~ kitty copy dolly puppy daisy penny baby party pinky

1. The <u>families</u> wrote <u>histories</u> to share with each other.

2.

3.

Test-Taking Skills

Fill in the circle next to the **plural y-ending** word that completes the sentence. (2 points each.)

1. All of our _____ have gone, the race is over.
   - Ⓐ jellies   Ⓑ worries   Ⓒ pets

2. Ring around the rosies, a pocket full of _____.
   - Ⓐ posies   Ⓑ ponies   Ⓒ pajamas

3. In the fall I love to pick _____ from the garden.
   - Ⓐ fairies   Ⓑ elves   Ⓒ berries

4. Sewing is one of my grandma's favorite _____.
   - Ⓐ cherries   Ⓑ hobbies   Ⓒ fruits

Integrated Activity

Use the **ies-ending** words from this page to create a word search. Write down all of the *ies*-ending words on a piece of paper. Count up all of the words and write the number on the back. Fill in the spaces between words with letters. Now, try to find all of your words between the letters on the page. (You could also have a friend try to find them!)

Core Curriculum Concept: Identifying plurals in isolation and their meaning, and using plurals in context; changing **y** to **i** and adding **es**.

Plurals: changing *f* to *v*

To make most words that end in **f** and **fe** plural, change the **f** to **v** and **add es**. For example, the plural form of the word **knife** would be **knives**.

Direct Activity

Using the rule above, make the following words **plural** and draw a picture to match the new words. (2 points each.)

1. leaf   leaves
2. loaf   _____
3. shelf   _____

1.

2.

3.

Writing Practice

Make the words below **plural**. Then write a silly story using those plural words and the three plural words above (*leaves*, *loaves,* and *shelves*). Circle the plural words in your story. (6 points.)

thief / thieves   calf / _____   elf / _____

As I was walking down the streets with (shelves) in my hands, I saw...

_____

_____

_____

Test-Taking Skills

Fill in the circle next to the correct **plural ending** for each word. (2 points each.)

1. life   Ⓐ lives   Ⓑ lifes   Ⓒ livs
2. half   Ⓐ halfs   Ⓑ halvs   Ⓒ halves
3. wife   Ⓐ wives   Ⓑ wifes   Ⓒ wivs
4. self   Ⓐ selfes   Ⓑ selvs   Ⓒ selves

Integrated Activity

Using an old magazine cut out all of the words ending in **f** or **fe** that you know. Glue them on a piece of paper and write down the plural form next to each word.

Core Curriculum Concept: Identifying plurals in isolation and their meaning, and using of plurals in context; changing **f/fe** to **v** and adding **es**.

Phonics—Grade 3—RBP0253   www.summerbridgeactivities.com   ©RBP Books

Irregular Plurals

To make some words **plural**, you need to change the spelling. For example, the plural for **tooth** is **teeth**, and the plural for **man** is **men**.

The singular and plural forms of some words are the same. The plural for **fish** is **fish**, and the plural for **sheep** is **sheep**.

Direct Activity

Draw lines to match the singular form of the word to its plural. (2 points each.)

1. child   feet
2. foot   mice
3. mouse   children

Writing Practice

Use the words below to complete the sentences below. Put the pairs of singular and plural forms on the same line. Put a line through the words you use. (2 points each.)

More than one __deer__ is __deer__,   woman...women

And more than one _____ is _____.   tooth...teeth

More than one _____ is _____,   ~~deer...deer~~

And more than one _____ is _____.   man...men

If more than one goose is geese,   sheep...sheep

Does that mean more than one moose is meese?   rice...rice

Test-Taking Skills

Fill in the circle next to the correct plural form of the word in parentheses ( ) in each sentence. (2 points each.)

1. These (child) love to read Harry Potter books!
   Ⓐ child   Ⓑ childs   ⊙ children
2. When the dentist looked at all of my (tooth), he said they looked great!
   Ⓐ tooth   Ⓑ teeth   Ⓒ tooths
3. In the spring it is time to sheer the (sheep) for their wool.
   Ⓐ sheep   Ⓑ sheeps   Ⓒ shoops
4. The field behind our house is full of (mouse).
   Ⓐ mouse   Ⓑ mousse   Ⓒ mice

Integrated Activity

Matching Game—Write down the singular form and plural form of all the words on this page on index cards (one word per card). Shuffle them and place them word side down in a pile on a table. Take turns with a partner turning two cards over at a time and try to match the singular with the plural. (See who can get the most matches!)

Core Curriculum Concept: Identification of irregular plurals in isolation and use of irregular plurals in context.

Plurals

Activity

Put an X over the incorrect plural forms and circle the correct plural forms. Then, uncover the phrase below by filling in each space with the underlined letter of each circled (or correct) plural. Put the underlined letter from the first circled plural in the first space, the letter from the next circled plural in the second space, etc. (The first two are done for you.)

W I _ _   _ _ _ _ _

_ _ _ _ es   _' _ ...

1. watch = (watches)
2. pile = (p_i_les)
3. thief = _t_hieves
4. chair = _c_hairs
5. foot = fee_t_
6. child = _c_hildren
7. deer = dee_r_
8. self = sel_f_es
9. goose = g_e_ese
10. pen = p_e_ns
11. woman = wo_m_ans
12. worry = _w_orries
13. story = stor_y_es
14. mouse = m_i_ce
15. sheep = _s_heep
16. tooth = teet_h_
17. calf = _c_alvs
18. berry = berr_i_es
19. box = bo_x_s
20. dish = _d_ishes

Core Curriculum Concept: Identification of plurals in isolation; use of plurals with **s**, **es**, **ies**, **ves**, and use of irregular plurals.

Phonics—Grade 3—RBP0253   www.summerbridgeactivities.com   ©RBP Books

Contractions

Contractions are two words that are shortened to make one word by leaving out a few letters. An **apostrophe** (') is put in the place of the missing letter or letters. For example, **is + not = isn't**, **we + are = we're**. (The word **won't** is an irregular contraction made from the words **will + not**.)

Direct Activity

Separate the **contractions** below into the two words they are made from. (2 points each.)

1. wasn't   was not _____
2. I'll   _____
3. we're   _____

Writing Practice

Make a **contraction** using the words below. Use each contraction in a sentence and put a triangle around it. (2 points each.)

1. did not   didn't   I didn't go out and play because I have a cold.
2. is not   _____   _____
3. she will   _____   _____

Test-Taking Skills

Fill in the circle next to the correct **contraction** made from the words below. (2 points each.)

1. will not   Ⓐ willn't   Ⓑ wiln't   Ⓒ won't   Ⓓ woln't
2. he will   Ⓐ hew'll   Ⓑ h'ill   Ⓒ he'ill   Ⓓ he'll
3. we will   Ⓐ we'll   Ⓑ wew'll   Ⓒ w'ill   Ⓓ we'ill
4. could not   Ⓐ couln't   Ⓑ couldn't   Ⓒ could't   Ⓓ cou'dnot

Integrated Activity

Using an old newspaper and your favorite crayon or marker, circle all of the **contractions** you can find. How many were there?

> Core Curriculum Concept: Forming contractions in isolation and using contractions in context.

Contractions

Direct Activity

Separate the **contractions** below into the two words they are made from. (2 points each.)

1. shouldn't _should not_
2. don't _____
3. wouldn't _____

Writing Practice

Make a **contraction** using the words below. Use each contraction in a sentence and put a rectangle around it. (2 points each.)

1. she is _she's_ She's my sister and my best friend.
2. has not _____ _____
3. I am _____ _____

Test-Taking Skills

Fill in the circle next to the correct **contraction** made from the words below. (2 points each.)

1. they are   Ⓐ they'r   Ⓑ the'are   Ⓒ th'are   ⬤ they're
2. he is   Ⓐ he's   Ⓑ h'is   Ⓒ hes'   Ⓓ his'
3. are not   Ⓐ ar'nt   Ⓑ aren't   Ⓒ arn't   Ⓓ ar'not
4. we have   Ⓐ we've   Ⓑ weh've   Ⓒ wehav'   Ⓓ we'v

Integrated Activity

Cut out three pictures from an old newspaper and glue them onto a sheet of paper. Write a "caption" below each picture using a contraction to describe what's going on. For example, below a picture of a girl crying you might write, "She's lost her cat."

Core Curriculum Concept: Forming contractions in isolation and using contractions in context.

Contractions

Direct Activity

Separate the **contractions** below into the two words they are made from. (2 points each.)

1. I've   I have
2. they'd   _____
3. she'd   _____

Writing Practice

Make a **contraction** using the words below. Use each contraction in a sentence and put a triangle around it. (2 points each.)

1. does not   doesn't   He doesn't know which toy he wants.
2. you have   _____   _____
3. did not   _____   _____

Test-Taking Skills

Fill in the circle next to the correct **contraction** made from the words below. (2 points each.)

1. you will   Ⓐ you'ill   🅑 you'll   Ⓒ youw'll   Ⓓ youll'
2. I had   Ⓐ I'd   Ⓑ Ih'd   Ⓒ I'ad   Ⓓ Id'
3. you are   Ⓐ you'r   Ⓑ you'ar   Ⓒ youar'   Ⓓ you're
4. where is   Ⓐ wher'is   Ⓑ where'is   Ⓒ wher's   Ⓓ where's

Integrated Activity

Cut out pictures from an old magazine. Glue them onto a piece of paper and write a sentence with a **contraction** below each picture. For example, below a picture of a bowl of soup you could write, "**It's** my favorite meal."

Core Curriculum Concept: Forming contractions in isolation and using contractions in context.

Contractions

Direct Activity

Separate the **contractions** below into the two words they are made from. (2 points each.)

1. what's   _what is_____
2. that's   _____
3. they've   _____

Writing Practice

Make a **contraction** using the words below. Use each contraction in a sentence and circle it. (2 points each.)

1. we would _we'd____   (We'd) like to help you put the dishes away.
2. it is   _____   _____
3. were not   _____   _____

Test-Taking Skills

Fill in the circle next to the correct **contraction** made from the words below. (2 points each.)

1. she would   Ⓐ she'd   Ⓑ sheh'd   © she'ad   Ⓓ shed'
2. they will   Ⓐ theyw'll   Ⓑ they'ill   © thew'll   Ⓓ they'll
3. you had   Ⓐ you'd   Ⓑ youh'd   © youd'   Ⓓ you'ad
4. they would   Ⓐ they'ld   Ⓑ theyw'd   © they'd   Ⓓ theyw'ld

Integrated Activity

Underline all of the **contractions** you find in an old magazine article. Then list them on a separate piece of paper and see if you can separate them into their original words. For example: **wasn't = was + not.**

> Core Curriculum Concept: Forming contractions in isolation and using contractions in context.

Contractions

Activity

Solve the crossword puzzle below by making each word or group of words into a contraction. Write them in the correct boxes below. (20 points.)

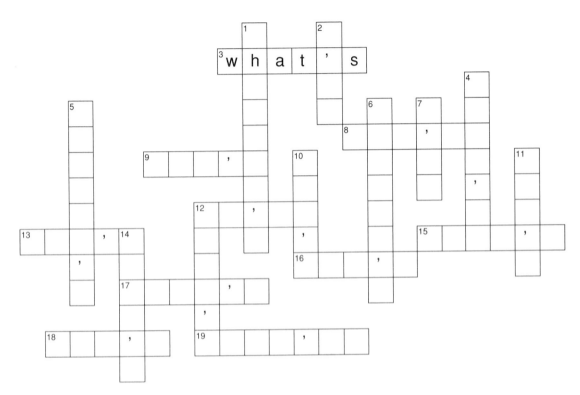

Across

3. what is   what's _____
8. you are _____
9. you had _____
12. we are _____
13. is not _____
15. they had _____
16. do not _____
17. are not _____
18. cannot _____
19. they will _____

Down

1. should not _____
2. I will _____
4. they have _____
5. could not _____
6. would not _____
7. I have _____
10. she had _____
11. will not _____
12. was not _____
14. that is _____

Core Curriculum Concept: Forming contractions in isolation.

Contractions

Activity

Find your way through the maze by connecting contractions that have been split into the correct words. Put an X through words that are not correct and circle the words that are correct. (20 points.)

Start

won't = wo + nt

can't = cannot

they're = they + are

hasn't = has + not

you've = you + have

aren't = ar + not

I'm = I + am

shouldn't = should + nt

don't = don + not

wouldn't = would + not

where's = where + is

she's = she + is

I'd = I + ad

doesn't = does + not

we've = we + have

you're = you + ar

hasn't = has + nt

I've = I + have

you'll = you + will

didn't = did + not

Finish

Core Curriculum Concept: Forming contractions in isolation.

Possessives: singular

For most words you add an **apostrophe** (') and an **s** to show ownership. For example, in the phrase "the cat's milk," the **'s** shows that the milk belongs to the cat.

Direct Activity

Add an **'s** to each word in the left column; then draw a line to the word in the right column that goes with the word in the left column. (2 points each.)

1. house_'s_   pond
2. Mom__   dress
3. frog__   window

Writing Practice

Rewrite each sentence using **possessives**. Circle the possessive word in each sentence. (2 points each.)

1. The purse that belongs to Mindy is red.
   (Mindy's) purse is red.
2. The food that belongs to the giraffe is mostly hay.

3. The video game that belongs to Adam is fun to play.

Test-Taking Skills

Fill in the circle next to the correct **possessive** use of the clues below. (2 points each.)

1. the puppy the girl owns   Ⓐ puppy's girl   ⬤Ⓑ girl's puppy
2. the rock the turtle has   Ⓐ turtle's rock   Ⓑ rock's turtle
3. the nest of the bird   Ⓐ bird's nest   Ⓑ nest's bird
4. the cookie that belongs to the baby   Ⓐ cookie's baby   Ⓑ baby's cookie

Integrated Activity

Look around the room and on the left side of a piece of paper list all of the items you see. Then, put an **'s** on the end of each word and write something that belongs to the object next to its name. For example: coat's button, shoe's lace, toy's handle … etc.

> Core Curriculum Concept: Forming singular possessives and using them in context.

www.summerbridgeactivities.com   Phonics—Grade 3—RBP0253

Possessives: singular

Direct Activity

Add an **'s** to each word in the left column; then draw a line to the word in the right column that goes with the word in the left column. (2 points each.)

1. sun_'s_ shell

2. turtle__ _rays

3. table__   chair

Writing Practice

Rewrite each sentence using **possessives**. Put a rectangle around the possessive word in each sentence. (2 points each.)

1. The candy belongs to Jenny.

   This is Jenny's candy.

2. This shoe belongs to Shelby.

3. This plant belongs to Mitchell.

Test-Taking Skills

Fill in the circle next to the correct **possessive** use of the clues below. (2 points each.)

1. the song the musician plays   Ⓐ musician's song   Ⓑ song's musician

2. the mirror that belongs to the lady   Ⓐ mirror's lady   Ⓑ lady's mirror

3. the eraser on this pencil   Ⓐ eraser's pencil   Ⓑ pencil's eraser

4. the lid that fits this bottle   Ⓐ bottle's lid   Ⓑ lid's bottle

Integrated Activity

Go on a nature walk and put small things from nature in a paper sack along the way. At home lay the items out on a table and tape each item to a heavy piece of cardboard. Next to each item write a **possessive** that shows where it came from. For example, if you found a stick by a tree you would tape the stick to the piece of cardboard and write "tree's stick" next to it.

> Core Curriculum Concept: Forming singular possessives and using them in context.

Possessives: plural

An **'s** is added to singular words to show ownership. To show ownership in **plural words ending in s,** you simply **add an apostrophe** ('). For example, if the toys belong to one cat, they would be the **cat's toys**. If the toys belong to many cats, they would be the **cats' toys**.

Direct Activity

Add an (') to each word in the left column; then draw a line to the word in the right column that goes with the word in the left column. (2 points each.)

1. friends'_____ ------------------------------------- engines
2. dogs_____   games
3. cars_____   bones

Writing Practice

Rewrite each sentence using **possessives**. Circle the possessive word in each sentence. (2 points each.)

1. The trees that belong to our neighbors are pine trees.
   Our (neighbors') trees are pine trees.
2. The beach balls that belong to the seals are wet.

3. The uniforms that belong to the soldiers are green.

Test-Taking Skills

Fill in the circle next to the correct **possessive** use of the clues below. (2 points each.)

1. the roses for the mothers   Ⓐ mothers' roses   Ⓑ roses' mother
2. the books the babies have   Ⓐ books' babies   Ⓑ babies' books
3. the rings the girls have   Ⓐ rings' girls   Ⓑ girls' rings
4. the tails on the pigs   Ⓐ pigs' tails   Ⓑ tails' pigs

Integrated Activity

Use clay or playdough to sculpt a scene using a pair of **possessives** from this page. For example, you could sculpt seals' beach balls or pigs' tails.

> Core Curriculum Concept: Forming plural possessives and using them in context.

Possessives: plural

Direct Activity

Add an **'** to each word in the left column; then draw a line to the word in the right column that goes with the word in the left column. (2 points each.)

1. rooms'___
2. bags___
3. lamps___

handles
shades
furniture

Writing Practice

Rewrite each sentence using **possessives**. Put a rectangle around the possessive word in each sentence. (2 points each.)

1. The plants in the gardens are blooming.

   The gardens' plants are blooming.

2. The pages of the books are numbered.

3. The wheels on the wagons are all black.

Test-Taking Skills

Fill in the circle next to the correct **possessive** use of the clues below. (2 points each.)

1. the branches on the trees   Ⓐ branches' trees   ⬤ trees' branches
2. the hands on the clocks   Ⓐ clocks' hands   Ⓑ hands' clocks
3. the keys that fit the doors   Ⓐ keys' doors   Ⓑ doors' keys
4. the buttons on the remotes   Ⓐ buttons' remotes   Ⓑ remotes' buttons

Integrated Activity

Draw a picture of your choice of **possessive** expressions from this page. For example: trees' branches, or rooms' furniture.

Core Curriculum Concept: Forming plural possessives and using them in context.

Possessives

Activity

Rewrite the clues below using possessives ('s or s'). Put the circled letters on the correct numbered lines to solve the mystery message. (2 points each.)

the leaves that belong to the trees

the arms that are on the octopus

the flippers that belong to the dolphin

the hat that belongs to the man

the socks that belong to the boys

the train that Steve has

the guppies that belong to the frogs

the bones that the dog has

the lock on the door

the rice that Wanda makes

1   2
Ⓣr ⓔⓔ s ' l Ⓔ a v ⓔ s

3 _ _ Ⓞ _ _ _ _ ' _ Ⓞ _ _ 4

5 _ Ⓞ _ _ _ _ _ ' _ _ _ Ⓞ _ _ _ _ 6

7 Ⓞ ' 8 Ⓞ _ _

9 _ Ⓞ _ _ ' _ Ⓞ _ _ _ 10

11 Ⓞ _ _ _ _ ' _ _ _ _ Ⓞ 12

_ _ _ Ⓞ ' Ⓞ _ _ _ _ _ 13 14

15 Ⓞ _ _ ' _ Ⓞ _ _ _ 16

_ Ⓞ _ _ ' _ _ _ Ⓞ 17 18

19 Ⓞ _ _ _ _ ' _ Ⓞ _ _ 20

___ ___ ___ ___   ___ ___ ___ k   ___ ___
13 3 9 15   19 5 4   16 12

t̲   ___ ___ s   b ___ ___ ___ ' s
1   8 20   17 10 18

___ ___ ___ e̲ ___ !
6 7 14 2 11

Core Curriculum Concept: Forming singular and plural
possessives and using them in context.

©RBP Books   www.summerbridgeactivities.com   Phonics—Grade 3—RBP0253

Possessives

Activity

Solve the crossword puzzle below by making each clue into a possessive expression. Write them in the correct boxes below. (20 points.)

Across

4. the cards that go with the games

g a m e s ' c a r d s

7. the ink in this pen

_ _ _ , _ _ _ _

8. the coats that fit the girls

_ _ _ _ _ ' _ _ _ _ _

9. the bananas at the store

_ _ _ _ _ ' _ _ _ _ _ _ _

10. the signs along the road

_ _ _ _ ' _ _ _ _ _

Down

1. the stamps on the letters

_ _ _ _ _ _ _ ' _ _ _ _ _ _

2. the light of the dawn

_ _ _ _ ' _ _ _ _ _

3. the petal of the rose

_ _ _ _ ' _ _ _ _ _

5. the trees in the forests

_ _ _ _ _ _ _ ' _ _ _ _

6. the stripes of the skunks

_ _ _ _ _ _ ' _ _ _ _ _

Core Curriculum Concept: Forming singular and plural possessives and using them in context.

Vowel Pairs: *oo* and *ew* digraphs

Vowel digraphs are vowels, and sometimes consonants, that come together to make a new sound. For example, the digraph **ew** in a word makes a sound like in the word **flew**. The digraph **oo** can make a similar sound, like in the word **noon**.

Direct Activity

Fill in the missing letters to complete the word. (2 points each.)

1. 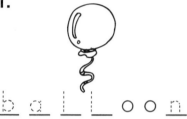   b a l l o o n

2.    __ __ e w

3.    __ o o __

Writing Practice

Make a word by adding letters to each **oo** or **ew**. Use the word in a sentence and circle it.
(2 points each.)

1. st oo l   Dad made a wooden (stool) for Mom's birthday. _____

2. __ ew   _____

3. __ oo __   _____

Test-Taking Skills

Fill in the circle next to the **oo** or **ew word** that makes sense in each sentence. (2 points each.)

1. My dad keeps his hammer and other _____ in the garage.
   Ⓐ wrenches   Ⓑ pools   Ⓒ screws   ⬤ tools

2. "Rocky the Rat" could be a ____ character.
   Ⓐ cartoon   Ⓑ few   Ⓒ new   Ⓓ loon

3. Last week we bought ___ shoes.
   Ⓐ goose   Ⓑ new   Ⓒ nice   Ⓓ blew

4. The _____ of workers took a break to eat lunch.
   Ⓐ loose   Ⓑ team   Ⓒ news   Ⓓ crew

Integrated Activity

Balloon Sentences—Gather five miniature balloons. Write fifteen **ew** and **oo** words on strips of paper and fold them up. Fill each balloon with three of the *ew* and *oo* words. Put air in each balloon and tie it up. Pop the balloons one at a time and use the words to make silly sentences. Keep going until you've popped all five balloons.

> Core Curriculum Concept: Sound-symbol association of words containing **oo** and **ew** digraphs, and use of those words in context.

www.summerbridgeactivities.com   Phonics—Grade 3—RBP0253

Vowel Pairs: *oo* and *ew* digraphs

Direct Activity

Draw a line to the **oo** or **ew** word that describes the picture. Put a rectangle around all of the *oo* and *ew* vowel pairs. (2 points each.)

1.

mouse
moose
goose
grew

2.

blew
brew
cloud
crew

3.

tool
table
school
room

Writing Practice

Write a silly sentence using at least six **oo** and **ew** words. Put a rectangle around all of the *oo* and *ew* words you used. You may use words from this page and the page before if you need help. (2 points each.)

A maroon raccoon flew over the lagoon in a new spoon.

_____

_____

Test-Taking Skills

Fill in the circle next to the letters that form a real **oo** or **ew** word. (2 points each.)

1. __ool	Ⓐ c	Ⓑ sp	Ⓒ f	● all of these
2. __ew	Ⓐ cr	Ⓑ x	Ⓒ z	Ⓓ none of these
3. __oon	Ⓐ n	Ⓑ s	Ⓒ m	Ⓓ all of these
4. __ew	Ⓐ d	Ⓑ a	Ⓒ x	Ⓓ none of these

Integrated Activity

Cartoons—Using the letters **oo** or **ew,** make a word such as *hoot*. Write that word in the middle of a blank sheet of paper and make a cartoon creature out of it to match the word.

> Core Curriculum Concept: Sound-symbol association of words containing **oo** and **ew** digraphs, and use of those words in context.

Phonics—Grade 3—RBP0253   www.summerbridgeactivities.com   ©RBP Books

Vowel Pairs: *au* and *aw* digraphs

When the vowel pairs **au** and **aw** are found in words, they usually make a sound like the sounds in the words **caught** and **law.**

Direct Activity

Fill in the missing letters to complete the word. (2 points each.)

1.   2.   3.

p a w   __ a w   __ a u n c h

Writing Practice

Make a word by adding letters to each **aw** and **au**. Use each word in a sentence. Circle the word. (2 points each.)

1. au to   The (auto) in the driveway wouldn't start. _____

2. __aw   _____

3. __aught   _____

Test-Taking Skills

Fill in the circle next to the **au** or **aw** word that makes sense in each sentence. (2 points each.)

1. Would you please turn on the kitchen ____?
   Ⓐ flaw   Ⓑ sink   ⒸＦ faucet   Ⓓ water
2. I think I've ___ a cold.
   Ⓐ caught   Ⓑ law   Ⓒ cop   Ⓓ got
3. The baby has just learned to ____.
   Ⓐ cry   Ⓑ kneel   Ⓒ roll   Ⓓ crawl
4. It is a perfect day for mowing the ____.
   Ⓐ lawn   Ⓑ grass   Ⓒ yard   Ⓓ haul

Integrated Activity

Launch a Word—With a partner write an **au** or **aw** word in crayon on a strip of paper. (Make sure your colors are different.) Sit on the floor with the crayon, a spoon, and strips of blank paper in front of you. Place a large bowl five feet away and set a timer for two minutes. Crumple up the first *au* or *aw* word and place it on the end of a spoon. When the timer starts, both of you "launch" the first word into the bowl. Keep writing and launching words until time runs out. Count how many *au* and *aw* words of each color landed in the bowl. The person with the most words in the bowl wins.

> Core Curriculum Concept: Sound-symbol association of words containing the vowel digraphs **au** and **aw**, and use of those words in context.

Vowel Pairs: *au* and *aw* digraphs

Direct Activity

Draw a line to the **au** or **aw** word that describes the picture. Circle all of the *au* and *aw* vowel pairs. (2 points each.)

1.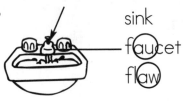

sink

f(au)cet

fl(aw)

2.

draw

write

art

3.

fawn

deer

caught

Writing Practice

Make up a silly sentence using at least six **au** and **aw** words. Circle the *aw* and *au* words you used. Use words from this page and the page before if you need help. (2 points each.)

(Saul) can (haul) all the (fawns) he (caught) on the (lawn,) before (dawn,) to the forest.

_____

_____

Test-Taking Skills

Fill in the circle next to the letter that forms a real **au** or **aw** word. (2 points each.)

1. __aul Ⓐ l Ⓑ t ●ⓒ h Ⓓ none of these

2. __aw Ⓐ j Ⓑ l Ⓒ s Ⓓ all of these

3. __aught Ⓐ c Ⓑ f Ⓒ p Ⓓ A and B

4. __awn Ⓐ d Ⓑ l Ⓒ f Ⓓ all of these

Integrated Activity

Jawbreakers— Write the word *jaw* on a chalkboard or white erase board. Break it apart by erasing the **j** and adding new letters to make a new **aw** word. Keep track of all the new words you make using tally marks. How many words did you make in all?

> Core Curriculum Concept: Sound-symbol association of words containing the vowel digraphs **au** and **aw**, and use of those words in context.

Vowel Pairs: *oi* and *oy* diphthongs

Diphthongs (dip-thongs) are two vowels that come together in words to make a new sound. The vowel pairs **oi** and **oy** make the sound in the words **coin** and **toy**.

Direct Activity

Fill in the missing letters to complete the word. (2 points each.)

1.
b o y

2.
__ o i __

3.
o y __ __ __ __

Writing Practice

Make a word by adding letters to each **oi** or **oy**. Use each word in a sentence. Circle the word. (2 points each.)

1. foil   Mom put (foil) over the food and placed it in the fridge.

2. __oi__   _____

3. __oy   _____

Test-Taking Skills

Fill in the circle next to the **oi** or **oy** word that makes sense in each sentence. (2 points each.)

1. The flower bulb should be covered with _____ when planted.
   Ⓐ soil   Ⓑ soy   Ⓒ dirt   Ⓓ toy

2. The old _____ we found will be valuable one day.
   Ⓐ money   Ⓑ quarter   Ⓒ coin   Ⓓ coy

3. If someone likes to _____ you, it is best to make them your friend.
   Ⓐ annoy   Ⓑ bother   Ⓒ boil   Ⓓ boy

4. The cake recipe asked for one third of a cup of ___.
   Ⓐ joy   Ⓑ oil   Ⓒ butter   Ⓓ egg

Integrated Activity

Dictionary Doozy—With a partner and a dictionary, think of an **oi** or **oy** word and look it up. (Don't let the other person see the definition.) Read only the definition to your partner. See if they can guess the correct *oi* or *oy* word. Take turns looking up definitions and guessing.

> Core Curriculum Concept: Sound-symbol association of words containing the diphthongs **oi** and **oy**, and use of those words in context.

Vowel Pairs: *oi* and *oy* diphthongs

Direct Activity

Draw a line to the **oi** or **oy** word that describes the picture. Put a rectangle around all of the *oi* and *oy* diphthongs. (2 points each.)

1.

hot
boil
foil
boy

2.

loud
toy
noise
music

3.

joy
join
glue
link

Writing Practice

Make up a tongue twister using at least six **oi** and **oy** words. Circle all of the *oi* and *oy* words you used. You may use the words from this page and the previous page if you need help. (2 points each.)

The boy Troy soiled a toy with boiling oil.

Test-Taking Skills

Fill in the circle next to the letter that forms a real **oi** or **oy** word. (2 points each.)

1. __oil   Ⓐ b   Ⓑ j   Ⓒ m   Ⓓ none of these

2. __oin   Ⓐ p   Ⓑ t   Ⓒ j   Ⓓ none of these

3. __oy   Ⓐ b   Ⓑ t   Ⓒ c   Ⓓ all of these

4. __oy   Ⓐ d   Ⓑ j   Ⓒ f   Ⓓ none of these

Integrated Activity

Vowel Pair Basketball—Write down at least ten **oi** and **oy** words on slips of paper. Use two paper cups for hoops. Label one *oi* and the other *oy*. Put the paper slips in a bowl and pick one to toss into a hoop. Aim for the hoop with the correct vowel pair. Continue playing until all ten words have been tossed. Empty the cups and count up your points (2 points for each vowel pair in the correct hoop). Try to get all ten words in the right cups.

Core Curriculum Concept: Sound-symbol association of words containing the diphthongs **oi** and **oy,** and use of those words in context.

Vowel Pairs: *ou* diphthong

When the diphthong **ou** is found in words, it usually makes an "ow" sound, as in the word **loud**.

Direct Activity

Fill in the missing letters to complete the word. (2 points each.)

1.

c l o u d

2.

__ o u __ __

3.

__ __ o u __

Writing Practice

Make a word by adding letters to each **ou** diphthong. Use each word in a sentence. Put a rectangle around the *ou* word. (2 points each.)

1. mouse   The mouse found a crumb on the kitchen floor.

2. __ou__   _____

3. __ou__   _____

Test-Taking Skills

Fill in the circle next to the **ou** word that makes sense in each sentence. (2 points each.)

1. The lemonade tasted too _____ to serve.
   Ⓐ scour   Ⓑ score   ⬤ sour

2. Please turn down the radio, it's too _____.
   Ⓐ noise   Ⓑ loud   Ⓒ talk

3. I just read a story about a lion and a _____.
   Ⓐ mouse   Ⓑ moose   Ⓒ move

4. Our family bought a comfortable new _____ to sit on.
   Ⓐ cot   Ⓑ couch   Ⓒ cold

Integrated Activity

Cloud Painting—Using a cotton-tip stick and cornstarch, "paint" as many **ou** words as you can think of on a piece of dark blue construction paper. The words will look like clouds in a bright blue sky!

> Core Curriculum Concept: Sound-symbol association of words containing the diphthong **ou**, and use of those words in context.

Vowel Pairs: *oo*

Sometimes the vowel pair **oo** makes a sound like that found in the word **book**.

Direct Activity

Fill in the missing letters to complete the word. (2 points each.)

1.

   _ O O _

2.

   _ O O _

3.

   _ O O _

Writing Practice

Make a word by adding letters from the list below to each **oo** . Use each word in a sentence and put a rectangle around it. (2 points each.)

w   h   g   st

1. _st_ood | I stood | in line and waited for my turn. _____

2. __ood   _____

3. __ood   _____

Test-Taking Skills

Fill in the circle next to the **oo** word that makes sense in each sentence. (2 points each.)

1. The wind ____ the leaves in the trees.
   - Ⓐ blew   ● shook   Ⓒ moved   Ⓓ hook

2. The shoe fit the girl's ___ perfectly.
   - Ⓐ book   Ⓑ feet   Ⓒ foot   Ⓓ toes

3. This meal was very ____.
   - Ⓐ good   Ⓑ nice   Ⓒ cook   Ⓓ tasty

4. The man ____ on the corner and waited for the bus.
   - Ⓐ look   Ⓑ sat   Ⓒ meet   Ⓓ stood

Integrated Activity

Hoop and Hook!—Write down all of the **oo** words from this page on index cards. Add some of your own if you'd like. Put a paper clip on the top of every card. Tie a magnet to a string; then put the word cards inside of a hula hoop or string ring on the floor. See how many *oo* words you can hook by swinging the string into the circle with the magnet!

Core Curriculum Concept: Sound-symbol association of words containing the vowel pair **oo**, and use of those words in context.

Vowel Pairs: *ow*

The vowel pair **ow** makes a sound like that in the word **how** as well as a **long o** sound as in the word **low**.

Direct Activity

Draw a line to the **ow** word that describes the picture. Circle all the *ow* vowel pairs.
(2 points each.)

1.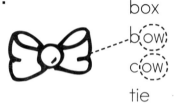

box
b(ow)
c(ow)
tie

2.

clown
crow
bird
blow

3.

mow
tower
flower
blossom

Writing Practice

Write a silly story using at least six **ow** words from the box below. Put a triangle around all the *ow* words you use. (6 points.)

Wow, did you hear that meow made by the...

Test-Taking Skills

Fill in the circle next to the letters that form a real **ow** word. (2 points each.)

1. __ow
   Ⓐ x   ⬤Ⓑ n   Ⓒ z   Ⓓ none of these

2. __own
   Ⓐ fr   Ⓑ l   Ⓒ n   Ⓓ all of these

3. __owel
   Ⓐ g   Ⓑ t   Ⓒ h   Ⓓ none of these

4. __ow
   Ⓐ l   Ⓑ m   Ⓒ t   Ⓓ all of these

Integrated Activity

Flower Show—Make flowers by cutting curvy circles out of colored construction paper. Write down as many **ow** words on the flowers as you can. (Write one word for each flower. Use each word only once.) With your flowers and some masking tape decorate your bike, a wagon, a scooter, or yourself like a float in a parade and show off your hard work! (You could do this with a friend and have a flower parade!)

> Core Curriculum Concept: Sound symbol association with words containing the vowel pair **ow**, and use of those words in context.

www.summerbridgeactivities.com
Phonics—Grade 3—RBP0253

Vowel Pairs: *ai, ay,* and *ei*

For most vowel pairs, remember that when two vowels go walking the first one does the talking. For example, think of the **ai** sound in the word **rain** and the **ay** sound in the word **pay**. (The pair **ei** also makes the **long a** sound when found in words.)

Direct Activity

Fill in the missing letters to complete each word.

(2 points each.)

1.

   s t a i n

2.

   _ _ a y

3.

   _ e i _

Writing Practice

Make a word by adding letters below to each **ai** and **ay**. Use each word in a sentence and put a triangle around it. (2 points each.)   spr   tr   p   s

1. spray   I like to spray the lawn, and my brother, with water. _____

2. __ail   _____

3. __ay   _____

Test-Taking Skills

Fill in the circle next to the **ai, ay,** or **ei** word that completes the sentence. (2 points each.)

1. Watch out for the ____ sticking out of the floor.
   - Ⓐ pail   Ⓑ rug   Ⓒ tack   ⬤ nail

2. Our horses love to eat ____.
   - Ⓐ may   Ⓑ hay   Ⓒ mice   Ⓓ straw

3. I can see every ____ in my hand when I make a fist.
   - Ⓐ crack   Ⓑ vein   Ⓒ line   Ⓓ veil

4. It is so much fun to sculpt things with ____.
   - Ⓐ clay   Ⓑ dough   Ⓒ hay   Ⓓ play

Integrated Activity

Using **ai, ay,** and **ei** words from this page write a play. You can even use *ai, ay,* or *ei* things as props in your play! Act out your play for your family, friends, or both!

> Core Curriculum Concept: Sound-symbol association with words containing the vowel pairs **ai, ay,** and **ei**, and use of those words in context.

Name _____   Date _____

Vowel Pairs: *ea* and *ee*

The vowel pairs **ea** and **ee** usually follow the rule: When two vowels go walking the first does the talking. The vowels **ea** and **ee** make the **long e** sound you hear in the words **bead** and **seen**. Sometimes **ea** makes the **short e** sound as in the words **bread** and **head**.

Direct Activity

Draw a line to the **ea** or **ee** word that describes the picture. Put a rectangle around all of the *ea* and *ee* vowel pairs. (2 points each.)

1.
feet
feather
leather
bird

2.
flea
tea
tip
hot

3.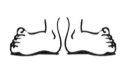
peel
feel
pet
feet

Writing Practice

Finish the silly story by using at least six **ea** and **ee** words from the box below. Cross each one out in the list as you use it. Circle all the *ea* and *ee* words in your story (6 points.)

| breath   meat   ~~beet~~   steam   head   street   cream   seat |

One day a huge (beet) came walking down the...

_____

_____

Test-Taking Skills

Fill in the circle next to the letters that form a real **ea** or **ee** word. (2 points each.)

1. __eat   Ⓐ h   Ⓑ s   Ⓒ b   ⬤ all of these
2. __een   Ⓐ c   Ⓑ s   Ⓒ f   Ⓓ none of these
3. __ead   Ⓐ c   Ⓑ thr   Ⓒ g   Ⓓ none of these
4. __eel   Ⓐ p   Ⓑ h   Ⓒ wh   Ⓓ all of these

Integrated Activity

A Meaningful Meal—Find a food in your kitchen with **ea** or **ee** in its name like *ice cream*, *wheat toast*, or *peeled oranges*, etc. Use that food to make a treat for a friend or family member. Fix it up nicely on a plate or in a bowl and take it to them with a note telling them how much they mean to you.

> Core Curriculum Concept: Sound-symbol association with words containing the vowel pairs **ea** and **ee**, and use of those words in context.

www.summerbridgeactivities.com   Phonics—Grade 3—RBP0253

Vowel Pairs: *oa* and *ou*

The vowel pairs **oa** and **ou** make the **long o** sound when found in some words, such as **float** and **dough**.

Direct Activity

Fill in the missing letters to complete each word. (2 points each.)

1.

o a _t_ s

2.

_ _ o u l d _ _

3.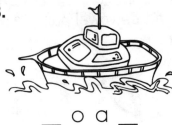

_ o a _

Writing Practice

Make a word by adding the letters below to each **oa** or **ou**. Use each word in a sentence and circle it. (2 points each.)

fl d ~~r~~ g

1. _r_ oad   This (road) will lead you home. _____

2. __ough   _____

3. __oat   _____

Test-Taking Skills

Fill in the circle next to the **oa** or **ou** word that makes sense in each sentence. (2 points each.)

1. I heard McKenzie come home, _____ I didn't see her.
   - Ⓐ load
   - Ⓑ but
   - Ⓒ since
   - ⬤ although

2. This _____ smells like vanilla when I wash with it.
   - Ⓐ soap
   - Ⓑ candle
   - Ⓒ coal
   - Ⓓ dough

3. I like to drink hot cocoa when I eat a _____.
   - Ⓐ cookie
   - Ⓑ doughnut
   - Ⓒ boar
   - Ⓓ cake

4. My brother got a pet _____ for his birthday.
   - Ⓐ moose
   - Ⓑ toad
   - Ⓒ snake
   - Ⓓ fish

Integrated Activity

Floating Dough—Using wooden popsicle sticks, write **oa** or **ou** words in permanent marker on each stick and glue them together to make two rafts. (Size doesn't matter, but they must be different shapes and you can only use sticks with *oa* or *ou* words on them.) Fill a sink or bowl with water. Using marble-sized pieces of play dough, see how much dough each raft will hold before it sinks.

> Core Curriculum Concept: Sound-symbol association with words containing the vowel pairs **oa** and **ou**, and use of those words in context.

Vowel Pairs: *ou*

The vowel pair **ou** can also make other sounds when found in words. Some examples of different **ou** sounds are found in the words **touch**, **group**, and **should**.

Direct Activity

Draw a line to the **ou** word that matches the picture. Write the word from the box below next to the picture that has the same *ou* sound. (2 points each.)

touch ~~group~~ should

1.

soap
soup
sour

__group__

2.

young
baby
enough

_____

3.

wouldn't
wood
couldn't

_____

Writing Practice

Finish the silly story using at least six **ou** words from the list below. Put a rectangle around all of the *ou* words you used. (2 points each.)

could   double   you   ~~couple~~   through   ~~southern~~   would   tour   touchdown   country

This southern couple _____

_____

_____

Test-Taking Skills

Fill in the circle next to the word that has the same **ou** sound. (2 points each.)

1. enough   Ⓐ touch   Ⓑ group   Ⓒ should

2. would   Ⓐ touch   Ⓑ group   Ⓒ should

3. you   Ⓐ touch   Ⓑ group   Ⓒ should

4. through   Ⓐ touch   Ⓑ group   Ⓒ should

Integrated Activity

Southern Sour Soup—Write down all the **ou** words from this page on strips of paper, crumple them up, and put them into a bowl. Write the words "Southern Sour Soup" across the top of a piece of paper. Take each bit of paper out of the bowl, read the word, and put it under the word on the paper with the same *ou* sound.

> Core Curriculum Concept: Sound symbol-association with words containing the vowel pair **ou**, and use of those words in context.

www.summerbridgeactivities.com   Phonics—Grade 3—RBP0253

Name _____ Date _____

Vowel Pairs

Activity

Find at least twenty words with vowel pairs in the word search below.

```
q s d d l u o h s q g i a q r y u s o a p k v l u
t k t s k o o b w g t e l m z m c e k f e o h e l
z a q e y y a l p o l e g e v v o n f e s a s u e
n y o b w z t c r f r n e n a d u o c e o d b s d
c o w l v d o u g h y c a l a d l u x t o a o c y
x z o k f p u k o o c z e e f r d g m f l o r a h
u l h n t k e v b y j m r d f i k h l n g r k u h
e n r n o o l l a b e b d s f g d o t l d n l g x
u i d t n e w s b f a y a m n p w x o y r c f h w
w o y u s w s s s o u p v e m e n o o l l m o t l
l c d o o t s w u a c t v b r y o n n a e a q s f
q a q d w l a l w a r c n l w f s k y l c g e e p
g b o o h x c i c n b w z n a l d p o a k q a o u
m c u c z o u l n m i o i u j l a u r d a t w k o
w l i n l o o t s o b a c m y i d t r l h p g o r
d f p a s l v k i o r e t u l j o a o e p u s o g
f d f k u i a f y s t q o h y o w o r b m g y h a
t w z a p y p x z e d x w w n q h x d l o z u s e
w y h c f l c r e w c f e s s c h s m m u i j f s
k a h l a k j y f e y y r a s d p l w p s p l l i
q r z w o q w h s w s b b r x o a o l t e m x a o
s p n o o i e a y t s u p p o s t o u c h s l w n
z s r d h a x s n b o o o n o x s o u r w v u y y
v c u o d x k x q f o a i h k o n w o l c e m y f
z j m j s h g u o r h t d l q o l v q z f t a y o
```

Write the words you find on the lines below. (20 points.)

_____   _____   _____

_____   _____   _____

_____   _____   _____

_____   _____   _____

_____   _____   _____

_____   _____

Phonics—Grade 3—RBP0253   www.summerbridgeactivities.com   ©RBP Books

R-Controlled Vowels: words with *ar*

Vowels followed by the letter **r** do not make short or long vowel sounds; instead, they make sounds of their own. When **ar** is found in a word, it makes a sound like in the word *star*.

Direct Activity

Write the word that each picture stands for; then put a rectangle around the **r-controlled** part of the word. (2 points each.)

1.
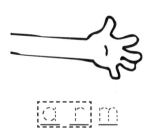

a r m

2.

— — — —

3.

— — — — — —

Writing Practice

Using all three lines, write your own pretend telephone conversation with as many **ar** words as you can. Put a rectangle around the **r-controlled** parts of the words. (6 points.)

Person 1: "Arnold, how do your arms feel?"

Person 2: "Sore from fixing the barn."

Person 1: "I'm glad I don't live on a farm!"

Person 1: _____

Person 2: _____

Person 1: _____

Test-Taking Skills

Fill in the circle next to the answer that tells about the **underlined vowel** in each word. (2 points each.)

1. h<u>a</u>t
   - Ⓐ short
   - Ⓑ long
   - Ⓒ r-controlled

2. l<u>a</u>te
   - Ⓐ short
   - Ⓑ long
   - Ⓒ r-controlled

3. p<u>ar</u>k
   - Ⓐ short
   - Ⓑ long
   - Ⓒ r-controlled

4. sh<u>ar</u>k
   - Ⓐ short
   - Ⓑ long
   - Ⓒ r-controlled

Integrated Activity

Create at least fifteen new words of your own that have the **r-controlled** part **ar** in them. Using your new "language" write a note to a friend. (Be sure to write what it really says on the back of the note.)

> Core Curriculum Concept: Identification of words with the **r-controlled vowel a**, as in the word *star*, sound-symbol association, and use of those words in context.

R-Controlled Vowels: words with *ar*

Direct Activity

Draw a circle around the correct name for each picture. (2 points each.)

1.
alarm
(lark)
bar

2.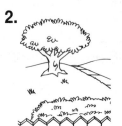
farm
arm
yard

3.
car
far
tar

Writing Practice

Make up a "knock-knock" joke using an **ar** word. Circle the *ar* words. (6 points.)

Knock, knock.
Who's there?
(Car.)
(Car,) who?
If you (car) about me, open
the door!

Knock, knock.
Who's there?
_____
_____, who?
_____
_____

Test-Taking Skills

Fill in the circle next to the **ar** word that completes the sentence. (2 points each.)

1. I would love to learn to play the _____.
Ⓐ ark   Ⓑ harp   Ⓒ piano

2. The "Big Dipper" is a constellation of _____.
Ⓐ mars   Ⓑ wars   Ⓒ stars

3. When we finish cleaning, the floors will _____.
Ⓐ shine   Ⓑ sparkle   Ⓒ hark

4. The weatherman will _____ us when a storm is coming.
Ⓐ warn   Ⓑ tell   Ⓒ alarm

Integrated Activity

Choose five made-up words with **ar** in them and write a made-up definition, or meaning, for each word.

> Core Curriculum Concept: Identification of words with the **r-controlled vowel a**, as in the word *star*, sound-symbol association, and use of those words in context.

R-Controlled Vowels: words with *ir*

When **ir**, **er,** and **ur** are found in words, they make a sound similar to the sound found in the words *sir*, *flower,* and *turn*.

Direct Activity

Write the word that each picture stands for, and then circle the **ir** part of the word. (2 points each.)

1.

t h ⓘ ⓡ d

2.

— — — —

3.

— — — — —

Writing Practice

Put a box around the word with an **r-controlled** vowel. Then use that word in a sentence and put a rectangle around it. (2 points each.)

1. tire ┆thirst┆ wire   After the hike I thought I would die of ┆thirst.┆

2. hire grill girl   _____

_____

3. squirrel squire squint   _____

_____

Test-Taking Skills

Fill in the circle next to the answer that tells about the **underlined vowel** in each word.
(2 points each.)

1. fl<u>i</u>p
Ⓐ short ●
Ⓑ long
Ⓒ r-controlled

2. fl<u>ir</u>t
Ⓐ short
Ⓑ long
Ⓒ r-controlled

3. d<u>ir</u>t
Ⓐ short
Ⓑ long
Ⓒ r-controlled

4. sh<u>ire</u>
Ⓐ short
Ⓑ long
Ⓒ r-controlled

Integrated Activity

For ten minutes write down all of the **ir** words you can think of and have a friend do the same. After ten minutes compare words. Put an X through all of the words that you both wrote down, circle the words that the other person does not have. Count who has the most *ir* words!

> Core Curriculum Concept: Identification of words with the **r-controlled vowel i**, as in the word *sir*, sound-symbol association, and use of those words in context.

www.summerbridgeactivities.com   Phonics—Grade 3—RBP0253

R-Controlled Vowels: words with *ir*

Direct Activity

Draw a triangle around the correct name for each picture. (2 points each.)

1.
swirl
△ girl △
twirl

2.
dirt
flirt
birch

3.
squirrel
squirt
sir

Writing Practice

Finish this short story using at least six **ir** words. Circle each *ir* word in the story. (6 points.)

Shirley, a flirty girl, liked to swirl and twirl in her dancing shirt and skirt...

_____

_____

_____

_____

_____

Test-Taking Skills

Fill in the circle next to the **ir** word that completes the sentence. (2 points each.)

1. My favorite ice cream flavor is Chocolate Fudge _____.
   Ⓐ ripple   ● swirl   Ⓒ squirt

2. The directions say to fill in the _____.
   Ⓐ box   Ⓑ circle   Ⓒ circus

3. I love to see the animals in the _____.
   Ⓐ circus   Ⓑ zoo   Ⓒ dirt

4. That kind of tree is called a _____.
   Ⓐ bird   Ⓑ birch   Ⓒ maple

Integrated Activity

On a large sheet of paper or on the pavement outside, use sidewalk chalk to draw pictures of as many **ir** words as you can.

Core Curriculum Concept: Identification of words with the **r-controlled vowel i**, as in the word sir, sound-symbol association, and use of those words in context.

www.summerbridgeactivities.com   ©RBP Books

R-Controlled Vowels: words with *er*

Direct Activity

Write the word that each picture stands for; then put a triangle around the **r-controlled** vowel part of the word. (2 points each.)

1.

g e r m s

2.

_ _ _ _

3.

_ _ _ _ _

Writing Practice

Write a pretend telephone conversation with as many **er** words as you can. Put a triangle around the **r-controlled** parts of the words. (2 points each.)

Person 1: "That person looked stern." _____

Person 2: "It's nicer that we jerked open the door for him."

Person 1: "Yea. I hope it helped him to feel better."

Person 1: _____

Person 2: _____

Person 1: _____

Test-Taking Skills

Fill in the circle next to the answer that tells about the underlined part of the word.
(2 points each.)

1. g<u>e</u>rm
   Ⓐ short
   Ⓑ long
   ⬤ r-controlled

2. g<u>e</u>m
   Ⓐ short
   Ⓑ long
   Ⓒ r-controlled

3. pap<u>er</u>
   Ⓐ short
   Ⓑ long
   Ⓒ r-controlled

4. sc<u>e</u>ne
   Ⓐ short
   Ⓑ long
   Ⓒ r-controlled

Integrated Activity

Cover a large plastic tray or cookie sheet with whipping cream; then use your finger to trace all the **er** words you can think of. You can lick your fingers clean after each word you write!

> Core Curriculum Concept: Identification of words with the **r-controlled vowel e**, as in the word *flower*, sound-symbol association, and use of those words in context.

www.summerbridgeactivities.com Phonics—Grade 3—RBP0253

R-Controlled Vowels: words with *er*

Direct Activity

Draw a rectangle around the correct name for each picture. (2 points each.)

1.
> tiger
> corner
> whisker

2.
> power
> eraser
> finger

3.
> sticker
> fern
> flower

Writing Practice

Make up a "knock-knock" joke using an **er** word. Circle the *er* words. (6 points.)

_____ Knock, knock. _____	_____ Knock, knock. _____
Who's there? _____	Who's there? _____
Corner. _____	_____
Corner, who? _____	_____ , who? _____
Did you want the corner _____	_____
the peas? _____	_____

Test-Taking Skills

Fill in the circle next to the **er** word that completes the sentence. (2 points each.)

1. In _____ icicles form on the tree branches.
   - Ⓐ January   Ⓑ summer   ⬤ winter

2. The hockey _____ scored three goals.
   - Ⓐ star   Ⓑ player   Ⓒ member

3. _____ to pick up bread at the store.
   - Ⓐ remember   Ⓑ try   Ⓒ whisper

4. The _____ rode his horse on the range.
   - Ⓐ cowboy   Ⓑ rancher   Ⓒ teacher

Integrated Activity

Jump rope to all of the **er** words you can think of. Count how many words you thought of.

> Core Curriculum Concept: Identification of words with the
> **r-controlled vowel e**, as in the word *flower*, sound-symbol
> association, and use of those words in context.

R-Controlled Vowels: words with *ur*

Direct Activity

Write the word that each picture stands for, then put a rectangle around the **r-controlled** part of the word. (2 points each.)

1.

c u r l

2.

— — — — — —

3.

— — — —

Writing Practice

Circle the word with an **r-controlled** vowel. Then use that word in a sentence and circle it.
(2 points each.)

1. tune   tunnel   (turn)   When you come to the corner, (turn) right.

2. pulse   purse   put   _____
                              _____

3. huge   hurt   hut   _____
                              _____

Test-Taking Skills

Fill in the circle next to the answer that tells about the **underlined vowel** in each word.
(2 points each.)

1. h<u>u</u>rl
   Ⓐ short
   Ⓑ long
   ⒸＲ r-controlled

2. cr<u>u</u>sh
   Ⓐ short
   Ⓑ long
   Ⓒ r-controlled

3. fl<u>u</u>te
   Ⓐ short
   Ⓑ long
   Ⓒ r-controlled

4. t<u>u</u>rkey
   Ⓐ short
   Ⓑ long
   Ⓒ r-controlled

Integrated Activity

Using clay, create five things that have **ur** in their names.

Core Curriculum Concept: Identification of words with the **r-controlled vowel u**, as in the word *turn*, sound-symbol association, and use of those words in context.

www.summerbridgeactivities.com   Phonics—Grade 3—RBP0253

R-Controlled Vowels: words with *ur*

Direct Activity

Circle the correct name for each picture. (2 points each.)

1.
(curtains)
curl
curse

2.
furnace
fur
furl

3.
turf
nurse
purr

Writing Practice

Finish this silly story using at least six **ur** words. Circle each **ur** word in the story. (6 points.)

A (turkey) was (curling) his (unfurled) feathers on his (turf) when he noticed something (furry) behind the (curtains.)

_____

_____

_____

_____

Test-Taking Skills

Fill in the circle next to the **ur** word that completes the sentence. (2 points each.)

1. I can tell when my cat is happy because she will _____.
Ⓐ paw   Ⓑ purse   ● purr

2. The wizard put a _____ on the mirror.
Ⓐ curl   Ⓑ curse   Ⓒ spell

3. Before the huge snowstorm we bought a new _____ to keep us warm.
Ⓐ fur   Ⓑ heater   Ⓒ furnace

4. _____ the flag so that we can put it up for Independence Day.
Ⓐ unfurl   Ⓑ open   Ⓒ turtle

Integrated Activity

Play "Eat your words!" Using alphabet cereal, make as many **ur** words as you can; then write them on a piece of paper. You can eat the words after you've written them down.

> Core Curriculum Concept: Identification of words with the **r-controlled vowel u**, as in the word *turn*, sound-symbol association, and use of those words in context.

R-Controlled Vowels: words with *or*

When **or** is found in a word, it also makes a sound of its own, as in the words *worm* and *fort*.

Direct Activity

Write the word that each picture stands for; then put a triangle around the **r-controlled** part of the word. (2 points each.)

1.

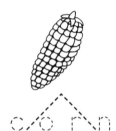

c͟o͟r͟n͟

2.

_ _ _ _

3.

_ _ _ _

Writing Practice

Write your own pretend telephone conversation with as many **or** words as you can. Put a rectangle around the **r-controlled** parts of the words. (6 points.)

Person 1: "C͟orly, would you o͟rder the o͟rchids for Flo͟ra?"

Person 2: "Those so͟rt of flowers are easily to͟rn."

Person 1: "You're right. I'll get the o͟range tulips instead."

Person 1: _____

Person 2: _____

Person 1: _____

Test-Taking Skills

Fill in the circle next to the answer that tells about the **underlined vowel** in each word. (2 points each.)

1. w<u>o</u>rk
Ⓐ short
Ⓑ long
● r-controlled

2. w<u>o</u>rd
Ⓐ short
Ⓑ long
Ⓒ r-controlled

3. sh<u>o</u>rt
Ⓐ short
Ⓑ long
Ⓒ r-controlled

4. h<u>o</u>t
Ⓐ short
Ⓑ long
Ⓒ r-controlled

Integrated Activity

With water-based markers and paper, write as many **or** words as you can. Then, using a paintbrush and water, trace over the words until they almost disappear.

> Core Curriculum Concept: Identification of words with the **r-controlled vowel o**, as in the word *worm*, sound-symbol association, and use of those words in context.

R-Controlled Vowels: words with *or*

Direct Activity

Draw a circle around the correct name for each picture. (2 points each.)

1.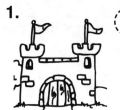
(fort)
fork
form

2.
storm
stork
story

3.
sports
shorts
sorts

Writing Practice

Make up a "knock-knock" joke using an **or** word. Circle the *or* words. (6 points.)

Knock, knock.
Who's there?
(Orange.)
(Orange,) who?
(Orange) you glad it's me!

Knock, knock.
Who's there?
_____
_____ , who?
_____
_____

Test-Taking Skills

Fill in the circle next to the **or** word that completes the sentence. (2 points each.)

1. It was so warm today that I put on my _____.
Ⓐ shorts   Ⓑ t-shirt   Ⓒ sport

2. I read the best _____ yesterday!
Ⓐ sort   Ⓑ book   Ⓒ story

3. Don't eat that apple because it has a _____ in it.
Ⓐ cork   Ⓑ worm   Ⓒ bug

4. When we visit my aunt's farm I love to ride the _____.
Ⓐ corn   Ⓑ horses   Ⓒ pony

Integrated Activity

Make a pile of rainbow-colored snacks (candies, cereal, fruit chews, etc.); then take out all of the colors with **r-controlled** vowels in their names.

Core Curriculum Concept: Identification of words with the **r-controlled vowel o**, as in the word *worm*, sound-symbol association, and use of those words in context.

Reading and Writing with Vowel Pairs and R-Controlled Vowels

Read the short story below, and then answer the questions.

Popcorn Clouds

Have you ever wondered what shapes you could find in a group of clouds on a summer day? The very best clouds to use while looking for art in the sky are curly rows of popcorn clouds. These are the largest, fluffiest, roundest clouds you can find. Sleek, coiled, and feather-like clouds won't work as well for shape finding. A good wind can loosen the clouds too much for truly great shape hunting. Go out on a calm day. The coolest place to go to spot popcorn clouds is the park or your yard on a warm summer afternoon. Find a large part of lawn, good for lying out on, and let your eyes wander to the sky. Your eyes are your tools for finding good cloud shapes. Once, I found cartoon characters that fought and then joined together to look like leaping horses. It's so easy to get caught up in the fun that it could get dark too soon! There is no need to worry about the clouds disappearing. Just about any day would make a super "popcorn cloud" finding day when it's summer! Take a crew of friends with you and work as a team. Try to find loads of new cloud drawings in the air. The greatest news would be to hear about how much you and your group of friends enjoyed the cloud-finding adventure!

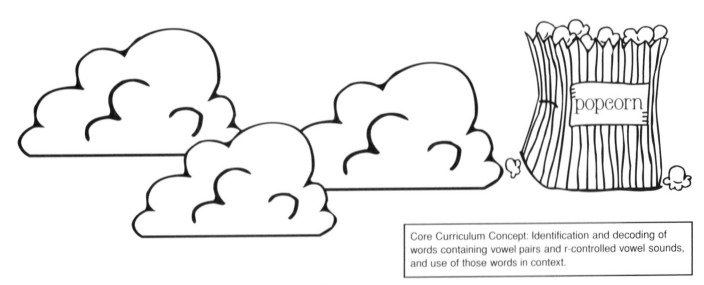

Core Curriculum Concept: Identification and decoding of words containing vowel pairs and r-controlled vowel sounds, and use of those words in context.

www.summerbridgeactivities.com Phonics—Grade 3—RBP0253

Reading and Writing with Vowel Pairs and R-Controlled Vowels

1. Fill in the circle next to the phrase that tells the main idea of the story. (1 point.)

   Ⓐ Finding clouds that look like cartoons.

   Ⓑ Having fun in the summer.

   Ⓒ Looking for "popcorn clouds."

   Ⓓ Doing things with your friends.

2. In a complete sentence use three words from the story to tell what "popcorn clouds" look like. (4 points.)

   _____

   _____

3. In a complete sentence use three words from the story to tell what kinds of clouds don't work as well for shape finding. (4 points.)

   _____

   _____

4. What **oo** word from the story tells what your eyes become when looking for clouds? (1 point.)

   _____

5. Write down five words from the story with vowel pairs in them. (5 points.)

   _____ _____ _____ _____ _____

6. Write down five r-controlled vowel words used in the story. (5 points.)

   _____ _____ _____ _____ _____

Prefixes: *un* and *dis*

Prefixes are letters that can be added to the beginning of words to change the meaning. The prefixes **un** and **dis** mean "not" or "the opposite of." For example, **happy + un = unhappy**, which means "not happy." And **like + dis = dislike**, which means "not like."

Direct Activity

Rewrite each word below, adding the correct prefix. Draw a picture of the new meaning for each word. (2 points each.)

1.

2.

3.

organize + dis = disorganize   tie + un = _____   lock + un = _____

Writing Practice

Rewrite each word below, adding the correct prefix, and use that word in a sentence.
(2 points each.)

1. agree + dis = _disagree_   Sometimes my friend and I disagree.

2. stitch + un = _____   _____

3. like + dis   = _____   _____

Test-Taking Skills

Fill in the circle next to the word that goes with each meaning. (2 points each.)

1. to take away color   Ⓐ discolor   Ⓑ dicolor   Ⓒ color

2. to undo wrapping   Ⓐ wrap   Ⓑ uwrap   Ⓒ unwrap

3. to lift a cover   Ⓐ uncover   Ⓑ ucover   Ⓒ cover

4. to break a connection   Ⓐ disconnect Ⓑ diconect   Ⓒ connect

Integrated Activity

Un/Dis Scavenger Hunt—Choose six words with the prefix **un** or **dis** from this page. Write them on a piece of paper. Search for examples of those words. For example, if one of the words on my list was *dislike*, I would look for something I don't like and write that word next to *dislike* on my page: *dislike onions*, etc. For a word like *uncover*, I would search for something I found uncovered. (You should not uncover something so you can write it down.) You can even play with a friend or family member and see who finishes first.

> Core Curriculum Concept: Sound-symbol association with words containing the prefixes **un** and **dis**, and use of those words in context.

Prefixes: *re*

The prefix **re** means "again." For example, the word **do** + **re** = **redo**, meaning "do again."

Direct Activity

Rewrite each word below by adding the prefix **re**. Draw a picture to show the meaning of each new word. (2 points each.)

1.

draw + re = _redraw___

2.

wind + re = _____

3.

try + re = _____

Writing Practice

Rewrite each word below, adding the **re** prefix, and use that word in a sentence. Put a rectangle around each prefix used. (2 points each.)

1. live + re   = _relive___   I'd love to [re]live my trip to Disneyland.

2. trace + re = _____   _____

3. invent + re = _____   _____

Test-Taking Skills

Fill in the circle next to the word that goes with the meaning. (2 points each.)

1. to open again   Ⓐ opened   ●Ⓑ reopen   Ⓒ unopened

2. to use again   Ⓐ disuse   Ⓑ reuse   Ⓒ used

3. to tell again   Ⓐ retell   Ⓑ untold   Ⓒ told

4. to write again   Ⓐ rewrite   Ⓑ unwrite   Ⓒ write

Integrated Activity

Re-Charades—Write down all the **re** words from this page on slips of paper. Fold them up and put them in a jar, bag, or bowl. Take turns with a partner choosing an *re* word. Act it out while the other person tries to guess the word.

> Core Curriculum Concept: Sound-symbol association with the prefix **re**, and use of those words in context.

Phonics—Grade 3—RBP0253   www.summerbridgeactivities.com   ©RBP Books

Prefixes: *pre*

The prefix **pre** means "before." For example, **pre + school = preschool**, which means "before school."

Direct Activity

Rewrite each word below by adding the prefix **pre**. Draw a line to the picture that goes with each new word. (2 points each.)

pay + pre = _prepay_   soak + pre = _____   test + pre = _____

Writing Practice

Rewrite each word below adding the **pre** prefix and use that word in a sentence. Put a triangle around each prefix used. (2 points each.)

1. score + pre = _prescore_ The judges prescore the contestants.
2. cook + pre = _____ _____
3. slice + pre = _____ _____

Test-Taking Skills

Fill in the circle next to the word that goes with the meaning. (2 points each.)

1. to send again   Ⓐ presend   Ⓑ unsend   ●Ⓒ resend
2. to paint before   Ⓐ repaint   Ⓑ prepaint   Ⓒ unpaint
3. to taste again   Ⓐ retaste   Ⓑ pretaste   Ⓒ distaste
4. to assign before Ⓐ unassign   Ⓑ reassign   Ⓒ preassign

Integrated Activity

Reci-**pre** Find—Choose a recipe book and write down all of the words with the prefix **pre** that you can find. How many were there?

> Core Curriculum Concept: Sound-symbol association with words containing the prefix **pre**, and use of those words in context.

Prefixes: *over*

The prefix **over** means "too much." For example, the word **fill + over = overfill**, meaning "to fill too much."

Direct Activity

Rewrite each word below by adding the prefix **over**. Draw a picture to show the meaning of each word. (2 points each.)

1. **2.** **3.**

flow + over = <u>overflow</u>   eat + over = _____   sleep + over = _____

Writing Practice

Rewrite each word below, adding the prefix **over**, and use that word in a sentence. Circle each prefix used. (2 points each.)

1. step + over = <u>overstep</u> Be careful not to (over)step the ledge.

2. do + over = _____ _____

3. load + over = _____ _____

Test-Taking Skills

Fill in the circle next to the correct meaning that goes with the word. (2 points each.)

1. overcorrect   Ⓐ correct again   Ⓑ correct before   ● correct too much

2. preview   Ⓐ to view before   Ⓑ to view again   Ⓒ to not view

3. unfair   Ⓐ fair before   Ⓑ too fair   Ⓒ not fair

4. overcook   Ⓐ cook too much   Ⓑ not cook   Ⓒ cook before

Integrated Activity

Over-Charades—Write down all the **over** words from this page on slips of paper. Fold them up and put them in a jar, bag, or bowl. Take turns with a partner choosing a word and acting it out while the other tries to guess the word.

> Core Curriculum Concept: Sound-symbol association with words containing the prefix **over**, and use of those words in context.

www.summerbridgeactivities.com   ©RBP Books

Prefixes: *mis*

The prefix **mis** means "badly." For example, the word **understood + mis = misunderstood** meaning "understood badly."

Direct Activity

Rewrite each word below by adding the prefix **mis**. Draw a line to the picture that best fits each word. (2 points each.)

1.    **2.**    **3.**

spell + mis = __misspell__   treat + mis = _____   understand + mis = _____

Writing Practice

Rewrite each word below, adding the prefix **mis**. Use that word in a sentence. Put a circle around the prefixes used. (2 points each.)

1. read + mis = __misread__   I (mis)read the directions for making cake.

2. lead + mis = _____   _____

3. place + mis = _____   _____

Test-Taking Skills

Fill in the circle next to the correct meaning that goes with the word. (2 points each.)

1. misrepresent   Ⓐ not represent   ⬤ represent badly   Ⓒ represent again

2. overstretch   Ⓐ stretch too much   Ⓑ stretch badly   Ⓒ stretch again

3. unkind   Ⓐ too kind   Ⓑ not kind   Ⓒ kind again

4. misfile   Ⓐ file again   Ⓑ not file   Ⓒ file badly

Integrated Activity

Look through the pages of your local newspaper and put a circle around every word you can find with the prefix **mis**. How many were there?

> Core Curriculum Concept: Sound-symbol association with words containing the prefix **mis**, and use of those words in context.

Prefixes

Activity

Write words for the definitions below using the prefixes in the key. Put the correct letters on the numbered lines to solve the mystery message. (2 points each.)

Key

un / dis =
not, take away

re =
again

pre =
before

over =
too much

mis =
badly, wrong

to take away color

to save again

to take out a bend

to paint again

to cook too much

to file badly

to take away the cover

to remove wrapping

to draw again

to sleep too much

T h ___ ___ ___ 's ___ ___   ___ ___ ___ ___ ___ ___ ___
      12 7 25   13 9   11 6 3 24 16 10 30

y _o_ _   a r e   _d_ ___ ___ ___ ___ ___ ___ ___ ___ ___ g
  21 5   1 23 20 14 19 4 22 17 27 29

t h e   ___ ___ ___ ___ ___ _r_ s!
        18 13 26 15 28 2

Core Curriculum Concept: Sound-symbol association with words containing the prefixes **un**, **dis**, **re**, **pre**, **over**, and **mis**, and use of those words in context.

Suffixes: *ful*

Suffixes are letters that can be added to the end of words to change the meanings. The suffix **ful** usually means "full of." For example, the word **help + ful = helpful**, meaning "full of help."

Direct Activity

Rewrite each word below by adding the suffix **ful**. Draw a line to the picture that best fits each word. (2 points each.)

1.    **2.**    **3.**

forget + ful = ~~forgetful~~   thought+ful=_____   thank+ful=_____

Writing Practice

Rewrite each word below, adding the suffix **ful**, and use that word in a sentence. Put a rectangle around the suffix used. (2 points each.)

1. play + ful   = playful   The puppy is very playful

2. wonder + ful = _____ _____

3. care + ful   = _____ _____

Test-Taking Skills

Fill in the circle next to the correct word that goes with the meaning. (2 points each.)

1. full of wishing	● wishful	Ⓑ wishful	Ⓒ wish
2. full of cheer	Ⓐ cheerful	Ⓑ cheerfull	Ⓒ cheery
3. full of peace	Ⓐ peacefull	Ⓑ peaceful	Ⓒ peace
4. full of color	Ⓐ colorfull	Ⓑ colorful	Ⓒ color

Integrated Activity

Thank-You Note—Write a thank-you note to someone. Use as many **ful** words from this page as you can. Send it when you are finished.

> Core Curriculum Concept: Sound-symbol association with words containing the suffix **ful**, and use of those words in context.

   www.summerbridgeactivities.com   Phonics—Grade 3—RBP0253

Suffixes: *less*

The suffix **less** means "without." For example, the word **friend + less = friendless**, which means "without friends."

Direct Activity

Rewrite each word below adding the suffix **less**. Draw a picture to show the meaning of each new word. (2 points each.)

1.  **2.**  **3.**

end+less = _endless_   home+less=_____   cloud+less=_____

Writing Practice

Rewrite each word below, adding **less**. Use each word in a sentence and circle the suffixes used. (2 points each.)

1. hope + less   = _hopeless_   The search for fun seemed hope(less.)
2. color + less   = _____   _____
3. sleep + less   = _____   _____

Test-Taking Skills

Fill in the circle next to the correct word that goes with the meaning. (2 points each.)

1. without fear   Ⓐ fearfull   Ⓑ fearfull   ● fearless
2. full of neglect   Ⓐ neglectfull   Ⓑ neglectless   © neglectful
3. without thought   Ⓐ thoughtfull   Ⓑ thoughtless   © thoughtful
4. full of power   Ⓐ powerless   Ⓑ powerful   © powerfull

Integrated Activity

Less-Painting—Choose a **less** word from this page and paint a picture to illustrate that word. Put the word in the title of your painting. For example, if I chose the word *cloudless*, I might paint a picture of a clear blue sky and the title of my painting could be "Cloudless Sky."

> Core Curriculum Concept: Sound-symbol association with words containing the suffix **less**, and use of those words in context.

Suffixes: *y* and *ly*

The suffixes **y** and **ly** are added to words to show how something is or in what way something is done. For example, the word *rainy* shows "how the day looks with rain." Or if something is done "softly," it is done "in a soft way."

Direct Activity

Rewrite each word adding the correct suffix. Draw a line to the picture that best fits each word. (2 points each.)

1.   **2.**   **3.**

curl + ly = _curly_   slow + ly = _____   luck + y = _____

Writing Practice

Rewrite each word below, adding **y** or **ly**. Use each word in a sentence and circle the suffixes used. (2 points each.)

1. quick + ly = _quickly_   The bird quick(ly) flew away.

2. might + y = _____   _____

3. soft + ly = _____   _____

Test-Taking Skills

Fill in the circle next to the correct word that goes with the meaning. (2 points each.)

1. nicely   Ⓐ in a nice way   Ⓑ not nice   Ⓒ very nice

2. graceful   Ⓐ a graceful way   Ⓑ full of grace   Ⓒ without grace

3. crispy   Ⓐ without crispness Ⓑ with crispness Ⓒ noisy

4. touchless   Ⓐ without touching   Ⓑ full of touch   Ⓒ a touching way

Integrated Activity

Y and **ly** Scavenger Hunt—List six **y** or **ly** words for this page. Looking around the house/yard/school see if you can find object examples of each word. Put the objects in a sack. For example, a curly ribbon, etc. (You can play with a partner to see who can find examples of all of the *y* or *ly* words first.)

> Core Curriculum Concept: Sound-symbol association with words containing the suffixes **y** and **ly**, and use of those words in context.

Suffixes: *able*

The suffix **able** means "can" or "can be." For example, the word **stretch + able = stretchable**, which means "can stretch." (With words that end in **e**, drop the **e** and add **able**. For example, l**ove + able = lovable**.)

Direct Activity

Rewrite each word adding the suffix **able**. Draw a line to the picture that best fits each word. (2 points each.)

1. 　　**2.** 　　**3.**

paint+able=<u>paintable</u>　　teach+able=_____　　read+able=_____

Writing Practice

Rewrite each word below, adding **able**. Use each word in a sentence and circle the suffixes used. (2 points each.)

1. live + able　=　<u>livable</u>　This house is very liv(able.)

2. stack + able =　_____　_____

3. like + able　=　_____　_____

Test-Taking Skills

Fill in the circle next to the correct meaning of each word. (2 points each.)

1. washable　　Ⓐ washing　　Ⓑ without　　● can be washed

2. sleepless　　Ⓐ without sleep　　Ⓑ can sleep　　Ⓒ in a sleepy

3. fixable　　Ⓐ can be fixed　　Ⓑ can't fix　　Ⓒ fix

4. richly　　Ⓐ richer　　Ⓑ can be rich　　Ⓒ in rich way

Integrated Activity

Grocery Store Scavenger Hunt—Make a list of each **able** word on this page. Take it with you to a grocery store and write down items that would fit each *able* word. For example, for the word *paintable*, you could write down eggs because eggs can be painted or colored. See how many examples you can find. You may even try to find two or three examples for each word!

> Core Curriculum Concept: Sound-symbol association with words containing the suffix **able**, and use of those words in context.

Suffixes: *ish*

The suffix **ish** means "like." For example, the word **fool + ish = foolish** means "like a fool." When adding **ish** to words ending in **e**, like *purple*, drop the **e** before adding **ish** (**purple + ish = purplish**). With words ending in a short vowel sound and one consonant, like *red*, double the consonant before adding **ish** (**red + ish = reddish**).

Direct Activity

Rewrite each word, adding the suffix **ish**. Draw a line to the picture that best fits each word. (2 points each.)

1.  **2.**  **3.**

self+ish= _selfish_   child+ish=_____   yellow+ish=_____

Writing Practice

Rewrite each word below, adding **ish**. Use each word in a sentence and circle the suffixes used. (2 points each.)

1. pink + ish   =   _pinkish_   The pink(ish) caterpillar wiggled away. _____

2. baby + ish   =   _____   _____

3. red + ish   =   _____   _____

Test-Taking Skills

Fill in the circle next to the correct meaning that goes with each word. (2 points each.)

1. brown–colored   Ⓐ brownful   🅑 brownish   Ⓒ brownable

2. in a sweet way   Ⓐ sweetly   Ⓑ sweetless   Ⓒ sweetish

3. sheep–like   Ⓐ sheepish   Ⓑ sheepy   Ⓒ sheepless

4. without meaning   Ⓐ meaningless   Ⓑ meaningful   Ⓒ meanly

Integrated Activity

Rainbow **Ish** Game—Colors are words that describe other objects, so they are very easy to add **ish** to. For example, a somewhat purple flower would be *purplish*. Take turns with a friend pointing to objects and having the other person describe the color by adding **ish**. For example, your friend might point to a tree, and you might either say "brownish" or "greenish," or both!

> Core Curriculum Concept: Sound-symbol association with words containing the suffix **ish**, and use of those words in context.

Suffixes

Activity

Rewrite the clues below using the prefixes in the key. Put the circled letters on the correct numbered lines to solve the mystery message. (2 points each.)

Key
ful = full of
less = without
y and ly = how something is or is done
able = can
ish = like

full of wishing

full of peace

can be washed

brown-like

without meaning

in a vibrant way

without thought

full of power

without odor

with clouds

$$\overset{1}{Ⓦ} \underset{}{i} \underset{}{s} \underset{}{h} \overset{2}{Ⓕ} \underset{}{u} \underset{}{l}$$

3 4 5   6
_ ◯◯ _ ◯ _ _ ◯

7 8   9
_ _ ◯◯ _ _ ◯

10 11 12
_ ◯◯ _ ◯ _ _ _

13   14   15 16
_ _ _ ◯ _ _ _ ◯ _ ◯◯

17 18   19
◯◯ _ _ _ _ _ _ ◯

20 21   22 23
_ _ ◯◯ _ _ ◯ _ ◯ _ _

24   25
_ ◯ _ _ _ ◯

26 27
_ ◯◯ _ _ _ _

28 29
_ _ _ _ ◯◯

W _ _ _ _ _ f _ _ !
1 24 13 26 5 10 2 21 14

_ _ _
19 11 25

_ _ _ _ _ _ t _ _ _
7 20 6 17 23 28   8 18 15

_ _
16 27

_ _ _ _ _ _ _ !
12 3 4 22 9 29

Core Curriculum Concept: Sound symbol association with words containing the suffixes **ful**, **less**, **y**, **ly**, **able**, and **ish**, and use of those words in context.

Reading and Writing with Prefixes and Suffixes

Read the short story below and then answer the questions.

Rainbow Recipe

To make a rainbow you will first need freshly gathered light. Find an uncut piece of sky and carefully prick one pin-sized hole directly below the sun. Allow the sky to reset and recut the hole. Collect the streaming light in a large seamless bucket and allow it to fill. In the bucket dissolve an unwrapped package of fluffy, feathery clouds and gently cover with shade. This will unlock the reddish, orangish, yellowish, greenish, bluish, and purplish colors. Be careful not to misplace the bucket! Allow the light and clouds to presoak, check for discoloring, and resoak in the cool shade. Uncover the bucket, do not worry if it is overflowing, and pretest with a spoon. The mixture should be thick, damp, and gray. Empty the thick gray mixture over a wide canyon and slowly let it hover overnight until it's heavy and cold. Your rainbow is almost ready. Gather one great flat stone and overlay the cloud to squeeze down all excess dampness. You can tap the stone with a roundish rock to release any droplets of rain. Watch as the grayness disappears. A sheer, unbreakable sheet of colors will be uncovered. Shake the sheet to release any extra dampness. Gently hang your newly made rainbow across a clothesline to make a bow. Lightly mist with spray to seal the colors. Allow it to re-dry. Your rainbow is now usable. Stand back and enjoy your colorful creation.

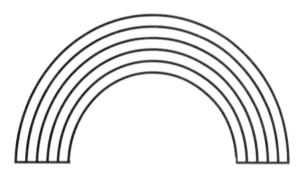

> Core Curriculum Concept: Identification and decoding of words containing prefixes and suffixes, and use of those words in context.

Reading and Writing with Prefixes and Suffixes

1. Fill in the circle next to the phrase that describes the main idea of the story. (1 point.)

   (A) How to bake a rainbow cake.

   (B) How to find a rainbow.

   (C) How to make rain.

   (D) How to make a rainbow.

2. In complete sentences write down the first three things from the story that you need to do to make a rainbow. (4 points.)

   _____

   _____

3. In complete sentences write down the last three things from the story that you need to do before your rainbow is ready. (4 points.)

   _____

   _____

4. In the story, what do you lie the rainbow across to make a bow? (1 point.)

   _____

5. Write down five words from the story with prefixes (un, re, dis, mis, pre, and over).
   (5 points.)

   _____   _____   _____

   _____   _____

6. Write down five words from the story with suffixes (ful, less, y, ly, able, and ish).
   (5 points.)

   _____   _____   _____

   _____   _____

Compound Words

Compound words are made by joining two smaller words together. For example, **water + fall = waterfall**.

Direct Activity

Connect each picture on the left with a picture on the right to make a real **compound word**. Write the compound word on the line below each picture. (2 points each.)

1. butterfly

2. _____

3. _____

Writing Practice

Draw lines to separate each **compound word** into smaller words. Then, write a silly definition using the smaller word parts. (2 points each.)

1. dragon|fly a fly that likes dragons _____

2. airport _____

3. cookbook _____

Test-Taking Skills

Fill in the circle beside the letter with the correct **compound word** made from the smaller words. (2 points each.)

1. snow and flake   Ⓐ flakesnow   Ⓑ snowlake   ⬤ snowflake

2. rain and bow   Ⓐ rainbow   Ⓑ bowrain   Ⓒ rainbo

3. room and bed   Ⓐ roombed   Ⓑ bedroom   Ⓒ bedrom

4. light and star   Ⓐ lightstar   Ⓑ starlight   Ⓒ starlit

Integrated Activity

Compound Collage—Break up the **compound words** on this page into smaller words. Using an old magazine, cut pictures of the smaller word parts and glue them together to make compound words. For example, for *butterfly* I would find a picture of butter and a fly and glue them side by side. Have a friend try to guess the compound words you've created!

Core Curriculum Concept: Identification of compound words and use of those words in context.

Compound Words

Direct Activity

Connect each picture on the left with a picture on the right to make a real **compound word**. Write the compound word on the line below each picture. (2 points each.)

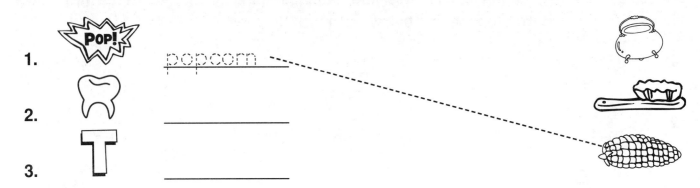

1. popcorn _____

2. _____

3. _____

Writing Practice

Draw lines to separate each **compound word** into smaller words. Then, write a silly definition using the smaller word parts. (2 points each.)

1. door|bell   a bell used to call doors to dinner. _____
2. footprint   _____
3. firehose   _____

Test-Taking Skills

Fill in the circle beside the letter with the correct **compound word** made from the smaller words. (2 points each.)

1. house and plant   Ⓐ planthouse   ⬤ houseplant   © houseplan
2. walk and side   Ⓐ sidewalk   Ⓑ walkside   © sidewak
3. hand and shake   Ⓐ handshak   Ⓑ handshake   © shakehand
4. case and brief   Ⓐ briefcase   Ⓑ briefcas   © casebrief

Integrated Activity

Take a friend and a pencil and piece of paper to the library. For ten minutes, write down all the book titles you can find with compound words in them. At the end of ten minutes see who found the most book titles.

> Core Curriculum Concept: Identification of compound words and use of those words in context.

Phonics—Grade 3—RBP0253   www.summerbridgeactivities.com   ©RBP Books

Syllables

Syllables are small parts that most words are made of. Every vowel sound in a word is a syllable of that word. For example, the word *tone* has one vowel sound, so it has one syllable. The word *birthday* has two vowel sounds, so it has two syllables.

Direct Activity

Fill in the vowel sounds for each picture. Say each name, count the **syllables** (vowel sounds) you hear, and write that number next to the picture. (2 points each.)

1.  ____   **2.**  ____   **3.**  ____

c o a t    f _ t h _ r   c _ t _

Writing Practice

Write a rap about words. Put in one **syllable** for each dot shown under the lines. (6 points.)

Word	up,	word	down,	mak–	ing	sounds.
•	•	•	•	•	•	•
A	E	I	O	U	and	Y.
•	•	•	•	•	•	•
Some	times	words	can	make	you	fly!
•	•	•	•	•	•	•
•	•	•	•	•	•	•
•	•	•	•	•	•	•
•	•	•	•	•	•	•

Test-Taking Skills

Fill in the circle next to the correct number of **syllables** in each word below. (2 points each.)

1. puppet   Ⓐ 2   Ⓑ 3   Ⓒ 1   Ⓓ none

2. log   Ⓐ 1   Ⓑ 2   Ⓒ 3   Ⓓ none

3. sidewalk   Ⓐ 3   Ⓑ 2   Ⓒ 1   Ⓓ none

4. downtown   Ⓐ 1   Ⓑ 2   Ⓒ 3   Ⓓ none

Integrated Activity

Take the rap that you wrote from this page and put it to music. Perform it for your family.

> Core Curriculum Concept: Identification of the number of syllables in words, division of 1- and 2-syllable words into syllable parts, and practical application of syllable usage.

Syllables

Direct Activity

Fill in the vowel sounds for each picture. Say each name, count the **syllables** (vowel sounds) you hear, and write that number next to the picture. (2 points each.)

1.  2

2.  ___

3. 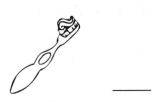 ___

d o g h o u s e   r _ _ n d r _ p   t _ _ t h b r _ s h

Writing Practice

Write a rap. Put in one **syllable** for each dot shown under the lines. (6 points.)

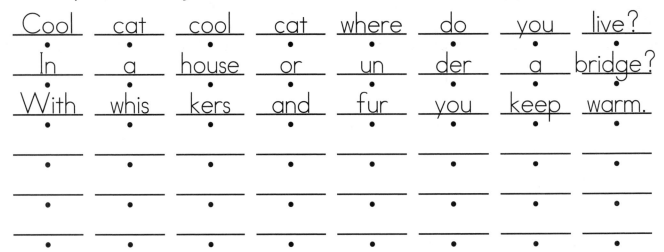

Cool   cat   cool   cat   where   do   you   live?
In   a   house   or   un   der   a   bridge?
With   whis   kers   and   fur   you   keep   warm.

Test-Taking Skills

Fill in the circle next to the correct number of **syllables** in each word below. (2 points each.)

1. snowflake   Ⓐ 3   ⬤Ⓑ 2   Ⓒ 2   Ⓓ none

2. wishbone   Ⓐ 2   Ⓑ 1   Ⓒ 3   Ⓓ none

3. notebook   Ⓐ 3   Ⓑ 2   Ⓒ 1   Ⓓ none

4. tray   Ⓐ 1   Ⓑ 2   Ⓒ 3   Ⓓ none

Integrated Activity

Family Math—Write down all of the names in your family. Count the syllables in each name and add them together. How many syllables make up your whole family?

> Core Curriculum Concept: Identification of the number of syllables in words, division of 1- and 2-syllable words into syllable parts, and practical application of syllable usage.

Syllables

Direct Activity

Fill in the vowel sounds for each picture. Say each name, count the **syllables** (vowel sounds) you hear, and write that number next to the picture. (2 points each.)

1.  _2_

l a d d e r

2.  ___

b _ t t _ r f l _

3.  ___

c _ n

Writing Practice

Write a poem about the words below. Use the number of **syllables** required for each line. This kind of poetry is Japanese and is called haiku. (6 points.)

Butterfly

(five syllables)   The/   bu/   tter/   fly/   floats,

(seven syllables)   ca/   tches/   the/   wind/   and/   dan/   ces

(five syllables)   le/   tting/   its/   wings/   glide.

Ladder

(five syllables)   _____

(seven syllables)   _____

(five syllables)   _____

Test-Taking Skills

Fill in the circle next to the word that has the correct number of **syllables**. (2 points each.)

1. 3   Ⓐ below   Ⓑ hole   Ⓒ earthworm   ● underground
2. 2   Ⓐ pancakes   Ⓑ toy   Ⓒ plate   Ⓓ syrupy
3. 3   Ⓐ friend   Ⓑ day   Ⓒ overflow   Ⓓ campground
4. 1   Ⓐ flashlight   Ⓑ lantern   Ⓒ campground   Ⓓ tent

Integrated Activity

Make Five—Think of a word that has two or three **syllables**. Tell that word to a partner. Your partner must try to say a word that has enough syllables in it to make five when added to your word. For example, if you say *popcorn* your partner will need to respond with a word that has three syllables, like *butterfly,* to make five syllables total. Keep taking turns until one person adds a word with the wrong number of syllables.

> Core Curriculum Concept: Identification of the number of syllables in words, division of 1- to 3-syllable words into syllable parts, and practical application of syllable usage.

Syllables

Direct Activity

Fill in the vowel sounds for each picture. Say each name, count the **syllables** you hear, and write that number next to each picture. (2 points each.)

1.  3

o v e r e a t

2.  ___

s k _ s c r _ p _ r

3.  ___

r _ n g

Writing Practice

Write a haiku poem on the lines below. Put the correct number of **syllables** on each line. (6 points.)

Ring

(five syllables)	My/	ring/	is/	shi/	ny,	
(seven syllables)	my/	ring/	was/	a/	spe/	cial/	gift.
(five syllables)	It's/	gold/	and/	gli/	tters.	

Skyscraper

(five syllables) _____

(seven syllables) _____

(five syllables) _____

Test-Taking Skills

Fill in the circle next to the word that has the number of **syllables** noted. (2 points each.)

1. 3   Ⓐ corner   Ⓑ butter   Ⓒ stand   ⬤ dragonfly
2. 4   Ⓐ counter   Ⓑ computer   Ⓒ librarian   Ⓓ books
3. 2   Ⓐ stream   Ⓑ sailboat   Ⓒ sail   Ⓓ boat
4. 1   Ⓐ bug   Ⓑ insect   Ⓒ puppy   Ⓓ kitten

Integrated Activity

Make up a haiku poem about your grandma, grandpa, or elderly neighbor. Write it in your best handwriting on a nice piece of paper and decorate it. Give it to that person as a special gift.

> Core Curriculum Concept: Identification of the number of syllables in words, division of 1- to 4-syllable words into syllable parts, and practical application of syllable usage.

(134)

Syllables

Direct Activity

Fill in the vowel sounds for each picture. Say each name, count the **syllables** you hear, and write that number next to the picture. (2 points each.)

1.  _3_

r o l l e r s k a t e

2.  ___

t _ l _ v _ s _ _ n

3.  ___

p _ _ n _

Writing Practice

Write a rap or a haiku poem on the lines below. (6 points.)

Rap

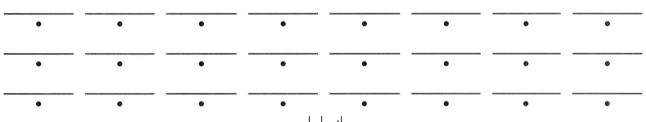

Haiku

(five syllables) _____

(seven syllables) _____

(five syllables) _____

Test-Taking Skills

Fill in the circle next to the correct **syllable** division in each word below. (2 points each.)

1. Ⓐ ju/mp/ing
    ⬤ jump/ing
    Ⓒ ju/m/pi/ng

2. Ⓐ fire
    Ⓑ fi/re
    Ⓒ f/i/re

3. Ⓐ te/ap/ot
    Ⓑ t/e/ap/ot
    Ⓒ tea/pot

4. Ⓐ with/out
    Ⓑ wi/tho/ut
    Ⓒ without

Integrated Activity

Sing your favorite song and clap to the syllables as you sing. For example:

    Ma   ry   had   a   lit   tle   lamb
    •   •   •   •   •   •   •

Now write your own words to the song. For example:

    Mo   ther   had   a   ba   by   boy
    •   •   •   •   •   •   •

Core Curriculum Concept: Identification of the number of syllables in words, division of 1- to 4-syllable words into syllable parts, and practical application of syllable usage.

Name _____ Date _____

Syllables

Activity

Find your way through the maze by connecting the words that have been broken up into the correct number of syllables. Put an X through the words broken up into syllables incorrectly and circle the words broken up into syllables correctly. (20 points.)

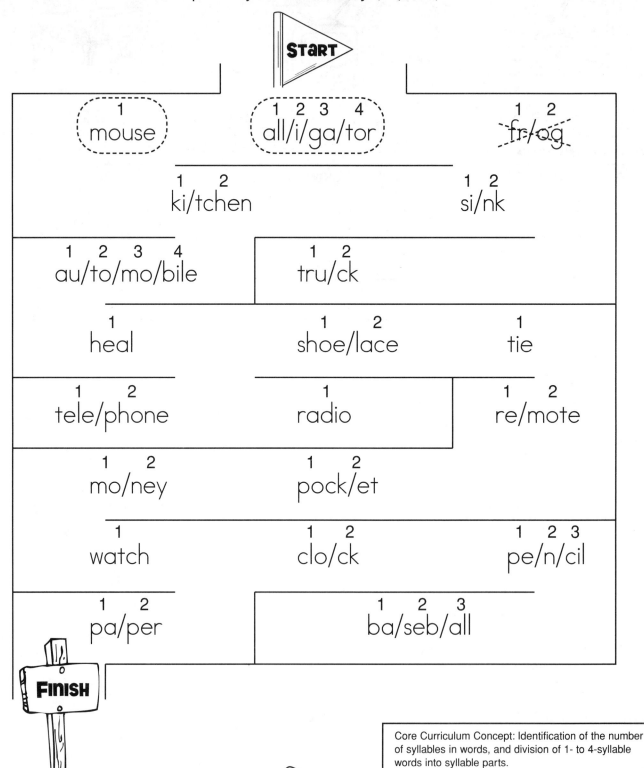

Alphabetical Order

A	B	C	D	E	F	G	H	I	J	K	L	M
N	O	P	Q	R	S	T	U	V	W	X	Y	Z

Alphabetical order means putting the words in the same order as the letters of the alphabet. Put words in alphabetical order by looking at the first letters of each word. If those letters are the same, look at the second letters. If those are the same, check the third letters and so on. For example, to put the words *stand*, *sorry*, and *stove* in alphabetical order, I would write them like this: (1) **s**orry, (2) **sta**nd and (3) **sto**ve.

Direct Activity

Write the name of each picture. Then, number them one through three in **alphabetical order**. (2 points each.)

1.    ___

   a p p l e

2.    ___

   ___ ___ ___

3.   ___

   ___ ___ ___ ___

Writing Practice

Rewrite the underlined words in **alphabetical order**. (6 points.)

Today I need to buy <u>flour</u>, <u>eggs</u>, <u>milk</u>, <u>sugar</u>, <u>oranges,</u> and <u>raisins</u>.

Today I need to buy _eggs_____, _____, _____, _____,

_____, and _____.

Test-Taking Skills

Fill in the circle above the list of words that are in **alphabetical order**. (2 points each.)

1. Ⓐ ● Ⓒ
   clam cap crow
   crow clam clam
   cap crow cap

2. Ⓐ Ⓑ Ⓒ
   plant pork pill
   pork pill plant
   pill plant pork

3. Ⓐ Ⓑ Ⓒ
   bat ball ball
   ball bat base
   base base bat

4. Ⓐ Ⓑ Ⓒ
   sing sang sung
   sang sing sang
   sung sung sing

Integrated Activity

Have your family, or a group of friends, line up and see if they can put themselves in **alphabetical order** by name. Check to make sure they are right!

> Core Curriculum Concept: Alphabetizing by first, second, and third letters.

Alphabetical Order

A	B	C	D	E	F	G	H	I	J	K	L	M
N	O	P	Q	R	S	T	U	V	W	X	Y	Z

Direct Activity

Write the word for each picture. Then, number them one through three in **alphabetical order**. (2 points each.)

1.  ___

   __television__

2.  __|__

   c

3.  ___

   d

Writing Practice

Rewrite the underlined words in **alphabetical order**. (6 points.)

Today I have to do <u>laundry</u>, <u>cleaning</u>, <u>errands</u>, <u>exercises</u>, <u>housework</u>, and <u>dinner</u>.

Today I have to do ___cleaning___, _____, _____, _____, _____, and _____.

Test-Taking Skills

Fill in the circle above the list of words that are in **alphabetical order**. (2 points each.)

1. Ⓐ   ⬤   Ⓒ
   hug   happy   hunt
   hunt   hug   happy
   happy   hunt   hug

2. Ⓐ   Ⓑ   Ⓒ
   giggle   gift   girl
   girl   giggle   giggle
   gift   girl   gift

3. Ⓐ   Ⓑ   Ⓒ
   jar   jail   jail
   jam   jar   jam
   jail   jam   jar

4. Ⓐ   Ⓑ   Ⓒ
   lock   lock   love
   lot   love   lock
   love   lot   lot

Integrated Activity

Pull out five of your favorite toys and line them up in **alphabetical order**. Write down the name of each toy on your list to make sure the order is right. Show a friend or family member how well you can organize!

> Core Curriculum Concept: Alphabetizing by first, second, and third letters.

138

Alphabetical Order

A	B	C	D	E	F	G	H	I	J	K	L	M
N	O	P	Q	R	S	T	U	V	W	X	Y	Z

Direct Activity

Write the word for each picture. Then number them one through three in **alphabetical order**. (2 points each.)

1. _____   hoop

2. _____   c_____

3. _____   h_____

Writing Practice

Rewrite the underlined words in this list of birthday gifts in **alphabetical order**. (6 points.)

I would like to give a doll, dog, dress, bow, box, and a ball to my sister for her birthday.

I would like to give a __ball__, _____, _____, _____, _____ and a _____ to my sister for her birthday.

Test-Taking Skills

Fill in the circle above the list of words that are in **alphabetical order**. (2 points each.)

1. Ⓐ   Ⓑ   ●
    hand harp hall
    hall hall hand
    harp hand harp

2. Ⓐ   Ⓑ   Ⓒ
    cart call cart
    call can   can
    can   cart call

3. Ⓐ   Ⓑ   Ⓒ
    ankle   ant   antler
    ant   ankle   ankle
    antler antler ant

4. Ⓐ   Ⓑ   Ⓒ
    bear   beam   beat
    beam   bear   beam
    beat   beat   bear

Integrated Activity

While your mom or dad is making dinner, ask if you can serve the different foods in **alphabetical order** on the plates. You could even ask other family members to watch you serve and try to guess what the pattern is!

Core Curriculum Concept: Alphabetizing by first, second, and third letters.

© RBP Books   www.summerbridgeactivities.com   Phonics—Grade 3—RBP0253

Alphabetical Order

A	B	C	D	E	F	G	H	I	J	K	L	M
N	O	P	Q	R	S	T	U	V	W	X	Y	Z

Direct Activity

Write the word for each picture. Then, number them one through three in **alphabetical order**. (2 points each.)

1.  ____

mitten

2.  ____

m

3.  ____

m

Writing Practice

Rewrite the underlined words in **alphabetical order**. (6 points.)

In the garden I found <u>lilies</u>, <u>lilacs</u>, <u>leaves</u>, <u>tulips</u>, <u>trees</u>, and <u>thorns</u> growing.

In the garden I found leaves, _____, _____, _____, _____, and _____ growing.

Test-Taking Skills

Fill in the circle next to the word that would come first in **alphabetical order**. (2 points each.)

1. Ⓐ small
   Ⓑ smaller
   Ⓒ smallest

2. Ⓐ bigger
   Ⓑ biggest
   Ⓒ big

3. Ⓐ took
   Ⓑ take
   Ⓒ talk

4. Ⓐ cook
   Ⓑ cake
   Ⓒ call

Integrated Activity

Alphabetical Service—Ask a parent or teacher if you can help them put items such as papers, books, music, movies, or toys in **alphabetical order** to help organize your house or schoolroom.

Core Curriculum Concept: Alphabetizing by first, second, and third letters.

Alphabetical Order

A	B	C	D	E	F	G	H	I	J	K	L	M
N	O	P	Q	R	S	T	U	V	W	X	Y	Z

Direct Activity

Write the word for each picture. Then, number them one through three in **alphabetical order**. (2 points each.)

1.  _____ _____
   bat

2.  _____ _____
   b

3.  _____ _____
   b

Writing Practice

Rewrite the underlined words in **alphabetical order**. (6 points.)

Some colors I've seen are <u>pink</u>, <u>purple</u>, <u>periwinkle</u>, <u>plum</u>, <u>puce</u> and <u>pine-green</u>.

Some colors I've seen are periwinkle, _____, _____, _____, _____ and, _____.

Test-Taking Skills

Fill in the circle next to the word that would come **last** in **alphabetical order**. (2 points each.)

1. Ⓐ small
   Ⓑ smaller
   ● smallest

2. Ⓐ took
   Ⓑ take
   Ⓒ talk

3. Ⓐ bigger
   Ⓑ biggest
   Ⓒ big

4. Ⓐ cook
   Ⓑ cake
   Ⓒ call

Integrated Activity

Empty a bag of animal crackers onto a table or plate and see if you can put them in **alphabetical order**. When you're finished, you can show a friend or family member and share your cookies with them.

Core Curriculum Concept: Alphabetizing by second and third letters.

www.summerbridgeactivities.com Phonics—Grade 3—RBP0253

Alphabetical Order

Activity

Uncover the picture below by coloring the numbers. Put the color names in alphabetical order to find out which color to make each number. (20 points.)

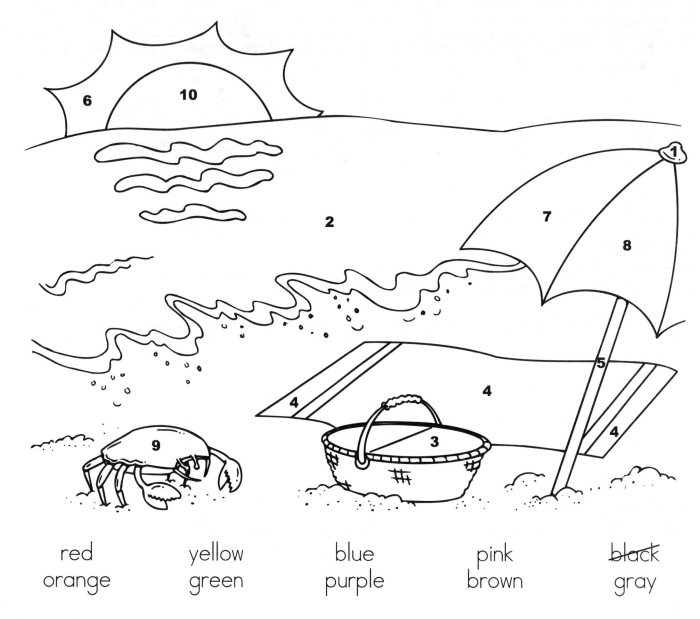

| red | yellow | blue | pink | black |
| orange | green | purple | brown | gray |

Colors in alphabetical order:

1. black   2. _____   3. _____   4. _____   5. _____

6. _____   7. _____   8. _____   9. _____   10. _____

> Core Curriculum Concept: Identification of the number of syllables in words, and division of 1- to 4-syllable words into syllable parts.

Antonyms

Antonyms are words that mean the opposite of each other. For example, the antonym (or opposite) of the word *short* would be *tall*.

Direct Activity

Finish writing the name of each picture then, draw a line from the picture on the left to its **antonym** on the right. (2 points each.)

1.  d a y

2. o _ _ n

3. h _ _ _ y

 c _ _ _ _ e

 s _ d

n i g h t

Writing Practice

Rewrite each sentence by replacing the underlined word with the correct antonym from the box. Circle the **antonyms**. (6 points.)

~~from~~	close
down	above

1. The flowers were sent <u>to</u> Aunt Lily.
   The flowers were sent (from) Aunt Lily.

2. Mike will <u>open</u> the doors at five o'clock.

   _____

3. The car is going <u>up</u> the hill.

   _____

Test-Taking Skills

Fill in the circle next to the **antonym** for each word. (2 points each.)

1. push   Ⓐ pull   Ⓑ press   Ⓒ open   Ⓓ none
2. sit   Ⓐ lay   Ⓑ rest   Ⓒ stand   Ⓓ none
3. wet   Ⓐ dry   Ⓑ soak   Ⓒ stain   Ⓓ none
4. frown   Ⓐ sad   Ⓑ mad   Ⓒ unhappy   Ⓓ none

Integrated Activity

Antonym Olympics—Write several activities you can do outside. Choose an "announcer." Contestants do the opposite of what the announcer says. For example, if the announcer says "Run to the fence and back," contestants walk to the fence and back.

Core Curriculum Concept: Identification of antonyms in isolation and in context.

    www.summerbridgeactivities.com   Phonics—Grade 3—RBP0253

Name _____   Date _____

Antonyms

Direct Activity

Finish writing the name of each picture. Then, draw a line from the picture on the left to its **antonym** on the right. (2 points each.)

1. 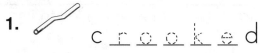 c _r_ _o_ _o_ _k_ _e_ d

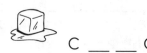 c _ _ d

2.  _ _ t

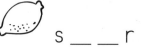 s _ _ r

3.  s _ _ _ t

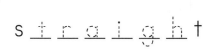 s _t_ _r_ _a_ _i_ _g_ _h_ t

Writing Practice

Rewrite each sentence by replacing the underlined word with the correct antonym from the box. Circle the **antonyms**. (6 points.)

asleep	front	~~dark~~

1. This room seems so <u>light</u>.

This room seems so (dark.)

2. Jacob was <u>awake</u> when I went downstairs.

_____

3. Please go to the <u>back</u> of the room.

_____

Test-Taking Skills

Fill in the circle next to the **antonym** for each word. (2 points each.)

1. run   Ⓐ jog   Ⓑ sprint   Ⓒ hop   ⬤ none
2. thick   Ⓐ fat   Ⓑ thin   Ⓒ wide   Ⓓ none
3. hungry   Ⓐ starving   Ⓑ wishing   Ⓒ fed   Ⓓ none
4. empty   Ⓐ zero   Ⓑ full   Ⓒ hollow   Ⓓ none

Integrated Activity

The Antonym Car Game—While you're traveling in the car or bus, look out the window and watch what's going on. Say the opposite of what you see going on. For example, if the cars are "stopped," say "going"; if a person is "walking," say "running"; if a tree is "waving in the wind," say "standing still." Try to find as many **antonyms** as you can.

> Core Curriculum Concept: Identification of antonyms in isolation and in context.

Phonics—Grade 3—RBP0253   www.summerbridgeactivities.com   ©RBP Books

Synonyms

Synonyms are words that mean the same thing as each other. For example, a synonym for *pretty* is *beautiful*.

Direct Activity

Finish writing the names of each picture. Then, draw a line from the picture on the left to its **synonym** on the right. (2 points each.)

1. h a p p y

 m _ _ _ e

2. f _ _ m

g l a d

3. f _ _ _ _ _ r

b _ _ _ _ _ _ m

Writing Practice

Rewrite each sentence by replacing the underlined word with the correct **synonym** from the box. Put a rectangle around the synonyms. (6 points.)

fast	speak
clean	

1. Will you <u>talk</u> to Dad for me?

   Will you ⸢speak⸥ to Dad for me?

2. Did you see that <u>quick</u> runner?

3. Will you <u>wash</u> the clothes in the hamper?

Test-Taking Skills

Fill in the circle next to the **synonym** for each word. (2 points each.)

1. big   Ⓐ large   Ⓑ small   Ⓒ short   Ⓓ none of these
2. shout   Ⓐ scream   Ⓑ yell   Ⓒ holler   Ⓓ all of these
3. listen   Ⓐ ignore   Ⓑ hear   Ⓒ deaf   Ⓓ none of these
4. trail   Ⓐ path   Ⓑ river   Ⓒ lake   Ⓓ all of these

Integrated Activity

Synonym Sounds—Take a walk outside with a friend. Listen to the sounds you hear. Choose one sound at a time and try to name all the things you can think of that make the same sound. Which sound had the most **synonyms**?

Core Curriculum Concept: Identification of synonyms in isolation and in context.

Synonyms

Direct Activity

Finish writing the name of each picture. Then, draw a line from the picture on the left to its **synonym** on the right. (2 points each.)

1. w <u>i</u> <u>n</u> d —————————  b <u>r</u> <u>e</u> <u>e</u> <u>z</u> e

2. s _ _ _ l c _ _ _ h

3. s _ _ a l _ _ _ _ e

Writing Practice

Rewrite each sentence by replacing the underlined word with the correct **synonym** from the box. Put a rectangle around the synonyms. (6 points.)

harm	~~gift~~
smile	

1. This <u>present</u> is for my brother.

   This ⌊gift⌋ is for my brother.

2. I love to make the baby <u>grin</u>.

   _____

3. Be careful not to <u>hurt</u> yourself.

   _____

Test-Taking Skills

Fill in the circle next to the **synonym** for each word. (2 points each.)

1. stir   Ⓐ glue   ⬤ mix   Ⓒ cook   Ⓓ none
2. give   Ⓐ take   Ⓑ steal   Ⓒ present   Ⓓ all
3. paint   Ⓐ cut   Ⓑ sew   Ⓒ color   Ⓓ none
4. make   Ⓐ create   Ⓑ invent   Ⓒ put together   Ⓓ all

Integrated Activity

Synonym Size—Look through a drawer or a shelf. Group the same sized items together. Record the groups on a piece of paper. For example, Group 1: marble, eraser, pen lid, etc; Group 2: staple, paper clip, penny, etc…

> Core Curriculum Concept: Identification of synonyms in isolation and in context.

Antonyms and Synonyms

Activity

Solve the crossword puzzle below by writing the **antonym** or **synonym** for each word. Write them in the correct boxes below. (20 points)

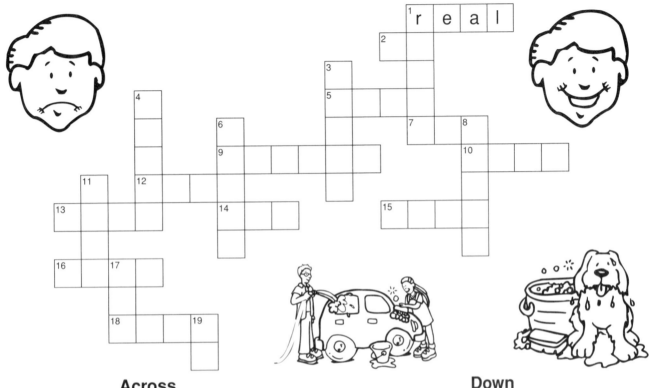

Across

1. antonym for fake _____ real _____
2. antonym for wait _____
5. antonym for kind _____
7. antonym for wet _____
9. synonym for small _____
10. antonym for under _____
12. synonym for pond _____ l a _ _ _____
13. synonym for kind _____ n _ c _ _____
14. synonym for question _____ a _ _ _____
15. antonym for thick _____
16. antonym for fast _____
18. antonym for up _____

Down

1. synonym for circle _____
3. antonym for big _____
4. antonym for frown _____
6. synonym for wash _____ _ _ e a n
8. antonym for old _____
11. antonym for won't _____
17. antonym for young _____
19. antonym for yes _____

Core Curriculum Concept: Identification of antonyms and synonyms in isolation.

Antonyms and Synonyms

Activity

To discover the phrase below, fill each space, in order, with the underlined letter of the correct **antonyms** and **synonyms**. Put an X over the incorrect answers and circle the correct answers. (20 points.)

I̲s the antonym for p̲ _ _ _ _ _
_ _ _ _ _ or _ _ _ _ ?

1. antonym of rich = (p̲oor)
2. synonym of stop = g̲o
3. antonym of water = fi̲re
4. synonym of love = hat̲e
5. antonym of calm = sti̲ll
6. antonym of sane = c̲razy
7. synonym of night = dar̲k
8. antonym of dark = l̲ight
9. antonym of awake = asle̲ep
10. antonym of take = stea̲l
11. antonym of quick = fas̲t
12. antonym of fast = s̲low
13. antonym of dry = w̲et
14. synonym of false = untru̲e
15. antonym of always = ne̲ver
16. synonym of close = shut̲
17. antonym of no = ye̲s
18. synonym of pre = befo̲re
19. antonym of smooth = bu̲mpy
20. antonym of before = afte̲r

Core Curriculum Concept: Identification of antonyms and synonyms in isolation.

Phonics—Grade 3—RBP0253   www.summerbridgeactivities.com   ©RBP Books

Homophones

Homophones are words that sound the same but are spelled differently and have different meanings. For example, the words *for* and *four* and *flower* and *flour* are homophones.

Direct Activity

Finish writing the names of each picture. Then, draw a line from the picture on the left to its **homophone** on the right. (2 points each.)

1. n _i_ _g_ _h_ t    c _ _ _ _ _ t

2. s _ n    k n _i_ _g_ _h_ t

3. c _ t    s _ n

Writing Practice

For each number, choose a pair of **homophones** from the box and use each one in a sentence. Circle the homophones. (2 points each.)

| ~~write~~ | too | tail | sea |
| ~~right~~ | two | tale | see |

1. _write_   I love to (write) poems.
   right   Turn (right) at the corner.

2. _____   _____

   _____

3. _____   _____

   _____

Test-Taking Skills

Fill in the circle next to the **homophone** that matches the word given. (2 points each.)

1. deer   Ⓐ fawn   Ⓑ door   ⬤ dear
2. wait   Ⓐ weight   Ⓑ say   Ⓒ stop
3. maid   Ⓐ to do   Ⓑ made   Ⓒ may
4. cent   Ⓐ sent   Ⓑ scent   Ⓒ A and B

Integrated Activity

Use pictures of **homophones** to write a message to a friend.

Would   you   write   a   letter?

Core Curriculum Concept: Identification of homophones.

Phonics—Grade 3—RBP0253   www.summerbridgeactivities.com   ©RBP Books

Homophones

Direct Activity

Draw a picture to show the meaning of each word in the **homophone** pairs below. (2 points each.)

1. week   weak   **2.** pale   pail   **3.** I   eye

Writing Practice

Write a sentence that goes with each picture. Then, write the **homophone** from the box that goes with that picture. Circle the homophone in each sentence. (2 points each.)

bare	beat	heel

1. The panda (bear) is holding bamboo. _____   bare

_____

2. _____   _____

3. _____   _____

Test-Taking Skills

Fill in the circle next to the **homophone** that matches the word given. (2 points each.)

1. need   Ⓐ want   ● knead   Ⓒ neat
2. pair   Ⓐ fruit   Ⓑ pain   Ⓒ pear
3. seam   Ⓐ seem   Ⓑ seat   Ⓒ sew
4. sell   Ⓐ buy   Ⓑ cell   Ⓒ send

Integrated Activity

Paint a silly picture of a pair of **homophones** from this page. For example, a pale pail or a bare bear. You may do as many as you'd like!

> Core Curriculum Concept: Identification of homophones and their meanings.

Homographs

Homographs are words that are spelled the same but mean different things. They can also have different sounds. For example, there is a *present* you give as a gift, or you can *present* a report to your class.

Direct Activity

Write the name for each picture; then draw a line from the picture on the left to the **homograph** on the right. (2 points each.)

1. t e a r _____   t e a r

2. w __ __ d    cl __ __ e

3. cl __ __ e    w __ __ d

Writing Practice

Copy the correct definitions from the list onto the lines below. (2 points each.)

to show the way   the wood on a tree trunk   a kind of metal
to bend down   the sound a dog makes   a tool used to shoot arrows

1. bow   to bend down
            a tool used to shoot arrows

2. bark   _____

3. lead   _____

Test-Taking Skills

Fill in the circle next to the correct name for each pair of words. (2 points each.)

1. lean / lean   Ⓐ homophone   ● homograph
2. bear / bare   Ⓐ homophone   Ⓑ homograph
3. for / four   Ⓐ homophone   Ⓑ homograph
4. all / awl   Ⓐ homophone   Ⓑ homograph

Integrated Activity

Picture Words—Write down all the **homographs** on this page on slips of paper and put them in a bowl. With a partner, some pencils, and drawing paper take turns choosing a homograph and drawing a picture of it. Have the other person try to guess the word from the picture you drew.

Core Curriculum Concept: Identification of homographs and their meanings.

Homographs

Direct Activity

Draw a picture to show the meaning of each word in the **homograph** pairs below. (2 points each.)

1. fence   fence   **2.** hand   hand   **3.** seal   seal

Writing Practice

Choose the correct **homograph** from the list to go with each set of definitions (meanings). Then, write a sentence using one meaning of that word. Put a rectangle around the homograph. (2 points each.)

~~score~~   fine   box

1. Ⓐ to slice into   _score_   The ⌐score¬ was five to four.
    Ⓑ the points in a game   _____   _____

2. Ⓐ a late fee   _____   _____
    Ⓑ a good feeling   _____   _____

3. Ⓐ a fighting sport   _____   _____
    Ⓑ a container   _____   _____

Test-Taking Skills

Fill in the circle next to the correct name for each pair of words. (2 points each.)

1. fair / fare   ● homophone   Ⓑ homograph
2. pant / pant   Ⓐ homophone   Ⓑ homograph
3. knead / need   Ⓐ homophone   Ⓑ homograph
4. sow / sow   Ⓐ homophone   Ⓑ homograph

Integrated Activity

Choose a pair of **homographs** from this page or the page before. Write a silly story and draw pictures to go with it. Your silly story could be about a "fencing fence" or a "box that boxes," etc.

> Core Curriculum Concept: Identification of homographs and their meanings.

www.summerbridgeactivities.com   Phonics—Grade 3—RBP0253

Reading and Writing with Antonyms, Synonyms, Homophones, and Homographs

Read the short story below and then answer the questions.

"A Backwards Fairy Tale"

When Sun Black met the seven giants, she told them that she **needed** a place to sleep. Sun Black was very happy because she had been running from the Good Stepdaughter. All day and all **night** she ran <u>while the wind made the trees wind around in circles</u>. When the seven giants heard the news, they decided to tell her to go away. Sun Black turned **pale** and <u>cried buckets of tears and wiped them with the tears in her dress</u>. She was so sad and unhappy because the giants had told her to leave. So, she found a chair to sleep in outside of the mansion where the seven giants lived. The seven giants were farmers and planted trees at night and rested and slept all day. When they came home to their mansion they found **Sun** Black putting dirt on **their** dishes and making oatmeal for dinner. Hooray! They screamed and yelled! They were so happy to see all that Sun Black had done! The next morning when the seven giants went to sleep, the Good Stepdaughter came to give Sun Black some tasty candy. The Good Stepdaughter was very pleased with Sun Black and wanted her to marry the Ugly Butler because <u>he could fence while standing on fences</u>. When Sun Black saw the Good Stepdaughter, she frowned and screamed "Go away!" and she **threw** the candy on the ground. So, the Good Stepdaughter went home and married the Ugly Butler herself, and Sun Black stayed at the seven giants' mansion. She put dirt on their dishes and **made** oatmeal and they all lived happily ever after!

Core Curriculum Concept: Identification of antonyms, synonyms, homophones, and homographs and their meanings in context.

Reading and Writing with Antonyms, Synonyms, Homophones, and Homographs

1. Fill in the circle next to the sentence that tells the main idea of the story. (1 point.)

   Ⓐ A handsome prince marries a lovely princess.

   Ⓑ Giants sleep all day and plant trees at night.

   Ⓒ A young girl finds a place where she can put dirt on dishes and live happily ever after.

   Ⓓ Giants are happy eating oatmeal for dinner.

2. In a complete sentence tell what three things Sun Black did when the giants told her she had to leave. (4 points.)

   _____

   _____

3. In complete sentences tell who the giants found when they came to their mansion. What two things was that person doing? (4 points.)

   _____

   _____

4. What did the Good Stepdaughter bring for Sun Black? (1 point.)

   _____   _____

5. Write down the seven **bold** words in the story next to their correct homophones below. (7 points.)

   Son _____, kneaded _____, knight _____, pail _____,

   there _____, through _____, maid_____.

6. What are the three underlined homograph phrases in the story? (3 points.)

   _____

   _____

   _____

Homophones and Homographs

Activity

Connect the dots by drawing lines to match the **homophones** and **homographs**. When the picture is complete use homophones to change the underlined words in the sentence below.
(20 points.)

pair read•
    for•

                    close•   •four
                     seal•   •close
                      box•   •seal
                      cot•   •box
                    lead•   •caught
                                            •lead

  write•   •right
    sea•   •see
   tear•   •tear
  wind•   •wind
   sun•   •sun
knight•   •night
   two•   •to

The read, white, and blew.
The _____, white, and _____.

pear red•

Core Curriculum Concept: Identification of homophones
and homographs and their meanings.

Name _____   Date _____

Guide Words

In a dictionary there are two words at the top of each page. These are called **guide words**. The guide word on the left side will be the first word on that dictionary page. The guide word on the right will be the last word on that page. To find the word you are looking for in a dictionary, use what you know about alphabetical order to find the two guide words that your word would come between. For example, if you were looking for the word *fit*, you would look on a page with the guide words crumb/hover.

Activity

Write the words from the list that would fit between each set of **guide words**. (Cross off the words that wouldn't fit at all). (20 points.)

~~abacus~~	ant	brick	butter	cream	crown	cut
dent	flip	hot	hut	icicle	kangaroo	lamp
lost	mall	map	nest	owl	push	quack
quaint	quiet	rake	stop	stuck	vampire	walrus

absent / crow

ant
_____

_____

_____

_____

crumb / hover

_____

_____

_____

_____

ice / lucky

_____

_____

_____

_____

man / put

_____

_____

_____

_____

quick / stun

_____

_____

_____

_____

Integrated Activity

Dictionary Chase—Use two dictionaries. Race a partner to see who can be the first to find every word in the box on this page. Play again with some words of your own.

Core Curriculum Concept: Use of alphabetical order for finding guide words.

Phonics—Grade 3—RBP0253   www.summerbridgeactivities.com   ©RBP Books

Guide Words

Activity

Using the five pairs of guide words, write the page number where each word could be found. (Cross off the words that wouldn't fit at all.) (20 points.)

aardvark / big p. 1   cat / elves p. 12   field / girl p. 28

gorilla / igloo p. 34   jump / last p. 39

1. caterpillar _____ p. 12 _____
2. fright _____
3. abyss _____
4. gosling _____
5. jury _____
6. karate _____
7. accept _____
8. fungus _____
9. lace _____
10. cave _____

11. galaxy _____
12. caution _____
13. gentleman _____
14. about _____
15. grade _____
16. catch _____
17. haiku _____
18. acid _____
19. lamb _____
20. iceberg _____

Integrated Activity

Dancing Dictionary—You need three or more people and a dictionary. Set a timer for one minute. Each person will take turns opening the dictionary, calling out a word, closing the dictionary, and passing it on. When the timer runs out, the person next to the one who just called out a word has to find that word in the dictionary. That person then has to take a paper clip. At the end of eight more rounds, the person with the least paper clips is the winner.

Core Curriculum Concept: Use of alphabetical order for finding guide words.

Letter and Sound Chart

A

hand   snake   rain   play   auto   jaw   star

C
  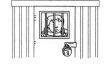 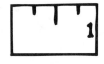 

cat   cell   inch   pack

E

ten   head   jeans   sheep   eight   person   stew

G
  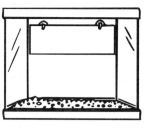 

gas   cage   cough

I

lip   stripe   pie   shield   girl

Letter and Sound Chart

U

cup

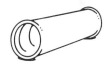
tube

burn

Y

sky

jelly

O

 mop   stone   boat   oil  balloon   hook popcorn

 mouse   dough   young   group   snow   owl   boy

Silent Consonants

knot

lamb

science

Consonant Digraphs

phone

fish

path

throw

Answer Pages

Page 5

Direct Activity
2. (qu)een   3. (z)ipper

Writing Practice
2. (c)andy   Sentences will vary.
3. (f)ork   Sentences will vary.

Test-Taking Skills
2. C   3. D   4. B

Page 6

Direct Activity
2. ha(t)   3. sig(n) or sto(p)

Writing Practice
2. we(b)   Sentences will vary.
3. be(d)   Sentences will vary.

Test-Taking Skills
2. B   3. C   4. D

Page 7

Direct Activity
2. (ch)air   3. (wh)istle

Writing Practice
2. Answers will vary, with *th* digraphs circled.
3. Answers will vary, with *ch* digraphs circled.

Test-Taking Skills
2. A   3. A   4. B

Page 8

Direct Activity
2. (th)   3. (ng)

Writing Practice
2. Answers will vary, with *ng* digraphs circled.
3. Answers will vary, with *th* digraphs circled.

Test-Taking Skills
2. D   3. C   4. A

Page 9

Direct Activity
2. photo, ——————
   cou(gh), (ph)oto, enou(gh)
3. telephone, ——————
   al(ph)abet, tele(ph)one, telegra(ph)

Writing Practice
Answers will vary. Any poem using *gh* and/or *ph* words.

Test-Taking Skills
2. A   3. B   4. A

Page 10

Direct Activity
2. ch, ~~chip~~   3. gh, ~~tough~~

Writing Practice
Any story using consonant digraphs and complete sentences with the digraphs circled.

Test-Taking Skills
2. A   3. B   4. D

   www.summerbridgeactivities.com   Phonics—Grade 3—RBP0253

Page 11

Direct Activity

2. pl　　　　**3.** gl

Writing Practice

2. Answers will vary, with the blends circled in the sentence.

3. Answers will vary, with the blends circled in the sentence.

Test-Taking Skills

2. C　　　　**3.** D　　　　**4.** C

Page 12

Direct Activity

2. fr　　　　**3.** bl

Writing Practice

2. Answers will vary, with the *cr* blends circled in the sentence.

3. Answers will vary, with the *br* blends circled in the sentence.

Test-Taking Skills

2. B　　　　**3.** A　　　　**4.** B

Page 13

Direct Activity

2. spr　　　　**3.** spl

Writing Practice

2. Answers will vary, with the *s* blends circled in the sentence.

3. Answers will vary, with the *s* blends circled in the sentence.

Test-Taking Skills

2. B　　　　**3.** D　　　　**4.** C

Page 14

Direct Activity

2. sk　　　　**3.** nd

Writing Practice

2. Sentences will vary, with all *mp* blends circled.

3. Sentences will vary, with all *nk* blends circled.

Test-Taking Skills

2. D　　　　**3.** D　　　　**4.** C

Page 15

Direct Activity

2. c r (a) b

3. r (a) b b i t

Writing Practice

Any poem that uses words with the short *a* sound with each short a sound circled.

Test-Taking Skills

2. A　　　　**3.** B　　　　**4.** C

Page 16

Direct Activity

2. t (e) n t

3. s (e) v (e) n

Writing Practice

Any riddles using words with the short *e* sound, with the short *e* sounds circle.

Test-Taking Skills

2. D　　　　**3.** A　　　　**4.** C

Answer Pages

Page 17

Direct Activity

2. s(i)ck   3. br(i)ck

Writing Practice

2. Answers will vary.
3. Answers will vary.

Test-Taking Skills

2. D   3. C   4. C

Page 18

Direct Activity

2. (o)ctopus 3. m(o)nster

Writing Practice

Any story using words with the short o sound with circles around them.

Test-Taking Skills

2. B   3. A   4. D

Page 19

Direct Activity

2. s(u)n   3. d(u)ck

Writing Practice

2. Answers will vary, with all short u sounds in sentence circled.
3. Answers will vary, with all short u sounds in sentence circled.

Test-Taking Skills

2. E   3. B   4. E

Page 20

Direct Activity

2. bench   3. apple

Writing Practice

2. Sentences will vary, with all short u sounds circled.
3. Sentences will vary, with all short i sounds circled.

Test-Taking Skills

2. D   3. B   4. D

Page 21 to 22

1. C
2. Wording will vary: Pat got wet and muddy from jumping in the puddles and dripped on the rug. So Pat's mom decided to get her a hat to stop her from getting wet.
3. Wording will vary: Pat loves to stomp in long puddles the best because the long puddles splash and make small puddles all around.
4. Wording will vary: The hat kept Pat from getting wet and muddy when she splashed. It made her very happy.
5. ă — Two of the following: Pat, hat, had, habit, splashed, plan, that, glad, happy, splash, and
   ě — Two of the following: wet, stepping, best, when, red, getting, went, fresh
   ĭ — Two of the following: skipping, dripping, habit, whistling, in, into, little, big, with, slick
   ŏ — Two of the following: hopping, mom, stomping, long, got, not, stop
   ŭ — Two of the following: puddle, duck, jump, muddy, rug,
6. Four of the following: jump, sing, whistle, walking, stepping, skipping, stomping, splashing.

www.summerbridgeactivities.com   Phonics—Grade 3—RBP0253

Answer Pages

Page 23

Direct Activity

2. c(a)ke   3. s n o w f l (a)k e

Writing Practice

Any poem that uses long *a* words and has circles around the long *a* sounds.

Test-Taking Skills

2. D   3. C   4. A

Page 24

Direct Activity

2. drawing/picture of a face
3. drawing/picture of grapes

Writing Practice

Any story using long *a* words with rectangles around them.

Test-Taking Skills

2. C   3. E   4. B

Page 25

Direct Activity

2. t(a)k e , t(a)p e
3. l(a)n e , l(a)k e

Writing Practice

2. Answers will vary. Triangle around long *a* word in sentence.
3. Answers will vary. Triangle around long *a* word in sentence.

Test-Taking Skills

2. D   3. C   4. C

Page 26

Students should have 20 of the following:

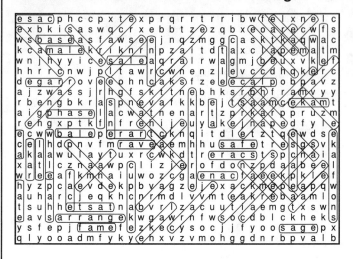

Page 27

Direct Activity

2. k(i)t e   3. h(i)v e

Writing Practice

Answers will vary. Any poem that uses long i words with circles around all of the long i sounds.

Test-Taking Skills

2. B   3. E   4. E

Page 28

Direct Activity

2. spine   3. stripes

Writing Practice

Answers will vary. Any story using long i words with the long i words underlined.

Test-Taking Skills

2. A   3. D   4. E

Answer Pages

Page 29

Direct Activity

2. sl[i]ce, r[i]ce ————————
3. tw[i]ne, l[i]nes, m[i]ce ———

Writing Practice

2-3. Answers will vary. Long *i* word circled in sentence.

Test-Taking Skills

2. A   3. B   4. D

Page 30

Students should have 20 of the following:

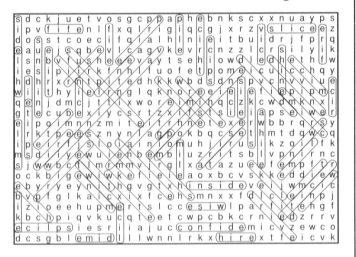

Page 31

Direct Activity

2. ph[o]ne   3. b[o]ne

Writing Practice

Answers will vary. Any poem using long *o* words with rectangles around the long *o* words.

Test-Taking Skills

2. D   3. B   4. D

Page 32

Direct Activity

2. drawing/picture of a hole
3. drawing/picture of a cone

Writing Practice

Any story using long *o* words with circles around them.

Test-Taking Skills

2. B   3. E   4. A

Page 33

Direct Activity

2. n[o]tes, n[o]se ————————
3. c[o]pe, b[o]ne ————————

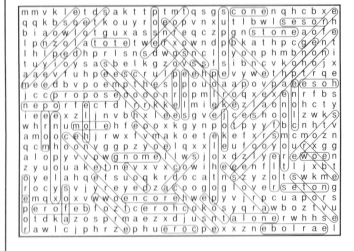

Writing Practice

2-3. Answers will vary. Long *o* words should be circled in sentences.

Test-Taking Skills

2. A   3. D   4. E

Page 34

Students should have 20 of the following:

www.summerbridgeactivities.com   Phonics—Grade 3—RBP0253

Answer Pages

Page 35

Direct Activity

2. m/u\e   3. c/u\be

Writing Practice

Any poem using long *u* words, with a triangle drawn around each of those words.

Test-Taking Skills

2. B   3. C   4. A

Page 36

Direct Activity

2. drawing/picture of a tube
3. drawing/picture of huge

Writing Practice

Any short story using long *u* words, with rectangles around them and complete sentences.

Test-Taking Skills

2. E   3. B   4. C

Page 37

Direct Activity

2. m/u\e, s/u\re, meas/u\re ———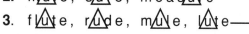
3. f/u\te, r/u\de, m/u\e, /u\te ———

Writing Practice

2-3. Answers will vary, with long u words circled in sentences.

Test-Taking Skills

2. E   3. A   4. C

Page 38

Students should have 20 of the following:

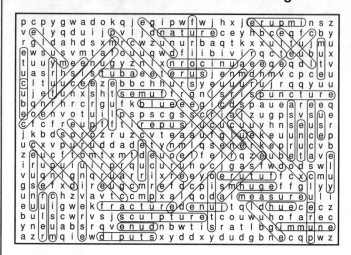

Page 40

1. D
2. Answers will vary. The boys wanted a change.
3. Answers will vary.
4. Answers will vary.
5. Answers will vary.

\ ā \

aching, amazed, faces, Blake, brave, change, crazy, Dane, day, flakes, Jake, James, lake, late, later, make(ing), maze, name, pane(s), place, play, raced, skate(ing), snaked, stay, take, trace, traced, waded, way

\ ē \

agreed, be, freezing, me, need, needed, scene, see, three, we

\ ī \

besides, bikes, find, fine, five, hide, ice, inside, nice, nine, outside, piles, piping, ride, time, while, white

\ ō \

awoke, cold, dove, drove, forged, frozen, go, holes, more, o'clock, over, phone, slopes, snow, so, sore, toes, window, wrote

\ ū \

amusing, excuse, huge, pictures, super, sure, tubes, you'd

6. dove, forged, waded, making, traced

Phonics—Grade 3—RBP0253   www.summerbridgeactivities.com   © RBP Books

Answer Pages

Page 41

Direct Activity
2. no   3. yes

Writing Practice
2. (sunny) Answers will vary, using [sunny] with a rectangle around it.
3. my̶ Answers will vary, using [my] with a rectangle around it.

Test-Taking Skills
2. A   3. A   4. A

Page 42

Direct Activity
2. no   3. yes

Writing Practice
2. Xed Answers will vary, using [crazy] with a rectangle around it.
3. circled Answers will vary, using [sly] with a rectangle around it.

Test-Taking Skills
2. A   3. A   4. B

Page 43

Direct Activity
2. drawing/picture of a fly
3. drawing/picture of lazy

Writing Practice
2. Answers will vary, using a long *e* y-ending word.
3. Answers will vary, using a long *i* y-ending word.

Test-Taking Skills
2. C   3. B   4. A

Page 44

Direct Activity
4. (silly)
5. (happy)
6. my̶
7. try̶
8. (rainy)
9. (sloppy)
10. spy̶
11. (crispy)
12. (story)
13. sky̶
14. by̶
15. (jolly)
16. why̶
17. pry̶
18. sly̶
19. (worry)
20. (frenzy)

Picture word answer
bunny

Page 45

Direct Activity
2. la̶x̶e
3. /c\amel

Writing Practice
2. cinema Answers will vary, using <u>cinema</u>.
3. (camera) Answers will vary, using <u>camera</u>.

Test-Taking Skills
2. C   3. B   4. B

©RBP Books   www.summerbridgeactivities.com   Phonics—Grade 3—RBP0253

Page 46

Direct Activity

2. ȼlown
3. bi[c]yȼle

Writing Practice

2. (lacy) Answers will vary, using *lacy*.
3. cⱥttle Answers will vary, using *cattle*.

Test-Taking Skills

2. B   3. C   4. B

Page 47

Direct Activity

2. △o r ⱥe
3. △rand

Writing Practice

2. (gasoline) Answers will vary, with *gasoline* circled.
3. ⱥiant Answers will vary, with *giant* circled.

Test-Taking Skills

2. D   3. C   4. A

Page 48

Direct Activity

2. ɡara△e
3. c r i n△e

Writing Practice

2. ☐George☐ Sentences will vary, with *George* in a rectangle.
3. dⱥagon Sentences will vary, with *dragon* in a rectangle.

Test-Taking Skills

2. B   3. C   4. A

Page 49

Direct Activity

4. (age)
5. gⱥs
6. (ice)
7. (nice)
8. (stage)
9. (giant)
10. (city)
11. (nice)
12. (huge)
13. (sage)
14. (giraffe)
15. (celery)
16. (trace)
17. clⱥp
18. (cent)
19. (plunge)
20. (cinnamon)

Picture word answer:

spaceship

Page 50

Students should have 20 of the following:

Answer Pages

Page 51

Direct Activity
2. wr   3. sc

Writing Practice
2. *kn* circled Sentences will vary, with *knock* circled.
3. *wr* circled - Sentences will vary, with *wrench* circled.

Test-Taking Skills
2. B   3. C   4. C

Page 52

Direct Activity
2. kn
3. wr

Writing Practice
Answers will vary.

Test-Taking Skills
2. C   3. C   4. B

Page 53

Direct Activity
2. mb   3. ck

Writing Practice
2. *c* circled Sentences will vary, with *thick* circled.
3. *gh* circled Sentences will vary, with *eight* circled.

Test-Taking Skills
2. C   3. C   4. B

Page 54

Direct Activity
2. mb
3. mb

Writing Practice
Answers will vary.

Test-Taking Skills
2. A   3. C   4. C

Page 55

Direct Activity
2. handed   3. hugged

Writing Practice
2. Answers will vary, with *ed* word circled in sentence.
3. Answers will vary, with *ed* word circled in sentence.

Test-Taking Skills
2. B   3. A

Page 56

Direct Activity
2. fried   3. scurried

Writing Practice
2. Answers will vary, with *ed* word circled in sentence.
3. Answers will vary, with *ed* word circled in sentence.

Test-Taking Skills
2. A   3. B   4. B

www.summerbridgeactivities.com   Phonics—Grade 3—RBP0253

Answer Pages

Page 57

Direct Activity

2. sliced   3. baked

Writing Practice

2. Answers will vary, with triangle around the *ed* word in the sentence.
3. Answers will vary, with triangle around the *ed* word in the sentence.

Test-Taking Skills

2. B   3. C   4. A

Page 58

Direct Activity

2. twisting   3. tapping

Writing Practice

2. Answers will vary, with rectangle around the *ing* word in the sentence.
3. Answers will vary, with rectangle around the *ing* word in the sentence.

Test-Taking Skills

2. C   3. A   4. C

Page 59

Direct Activity

2. skating   3. driving

Writing Practice

2. Answers will vary, with circle around the *ing* word in the sentence.
3. Answers will vary, with circle around the *ing* word in the sentence.

Test-Taking Skills

2. A   3. B   4. C

Page 60

Direct Activity

2. staked   3. spied

Writing Practice

2. Answers will vary, with triangle around the *ing* word in the sentence.
3. Answers will vary, with triangle around the *ing* word in the sentence.

Test-Taking Skills

2. A   3. C   4. B

Page 61

Direct Activity

2. studies   3. cooks

Writing Practice

2. Answers will vary, with rectangle around the *s*-ending word in the sentence.
3. Answers will vary, with rectangle around the *s*-ending word in the sentence.

Test-Taking Skills

2. B   3. A   4. C

Page 62

Direct Activity

2. buses   3. brushes

Writing Practice

2. mixes, hisses, pushes, misses, boxes, watches, faxes
3. Sentences will vary, with triangles around *es* words.

Test-Taking Skills

2. C   3. A   4. B

170

Answer Pages

Page 63

Direct Activity
2. sing   3. fish

Writing Practice
2. Answers will vary, with a circle around the *ing* word in the sentence.
3. Answers will vary, with a circle around the *ed* word in the sentence.

Test-Taking Skills
2. C   3. C   4. A

Page 64

Direct Activity
Start ⟶ spying ⟶ hugged ⟶ catches ⟶ bake ⟶ tries ⟶ pat ⟶ sings ⟶ pointed ⟶ race ⟶ studying ⟶ jogs ⟶ Finish.

Page 65

Direct Activity
2. cheaper   3. thicker

Writing Practice
2. Answers will vary, with a circle around the *er* word in the sentence.
3. Answers will vary, with a circle around the *er* word in the sentence.

Test-Taking Skills
2. B   3. C   4. A

Page 66

Direct Activity
2. youngest   3. tallest

Writing Practice
2. Answers will vary, with a circle around the *est* word in the sentence.
3. Answers will vary, with a circle around the *est* word in the sentence.

Test-Taking Skills
2. A   3. C   4. A

Page 67

Direct Activity
2. lovelier, loveliest
3. bubblier, bubbliest

Writing Practice
Answers will vary, with rectangles around the *er* words and circles around the *est* words.

Test-Taking Skills
2. A   3. B   4. B

Page 68

Direct Activity
2. wetter, wettest
3. fatter, fattest

Writing Practice
2. Answers will vary, with a circle around the *er* word in the sentence.
3. Answers will vary, with a circle around the *est* word in the sentence.

Test-Taking Skills
2. C   3. A   4. C

    www.summerbridgeactivities.com   Phonics—Grade 3—RBP0253

Page 69

Direct Activity

2. nice　　　　　3. wise

Writing Practice

2. Answers will vary, with a rectangle around the *est* word in the sentence.
3. Answers will vary, with a circle around the *er* word in the sentence.

Test-Taking Skills

2. C　　　3. B　　　4. C

Page 70

Direct Activity

2. coldest
3. uglier
4. reddest
5. earliest
6. younger
7. tiniest
8. fastiest
9. harder
10. newer
11. prettier
12. biggest
13. truer
14. healthier
15. wettest
16. smallest
17. tightest
18. messier
19. wiser
20. quietest

Mystery phrase answer

You're the greatest!

Page 71

Direct Activity

2. cans　　　　　3. piles

Writing Practice

pears, pickles, eggs, apples, rolls, oranges

Test-Taking Skills

2. C　　　3. C　　　4. B

Page 72

Direct Activity

2. branches
3. kisses

Writing Practice

dishes, grasses, buses, finches, watches, faxes

Test-Taking Skills

2. A　　　3. C　　　4. B

Page 73

Direct Activity

2. stories
3. bunnies

Writing Practice

2. Answers will vary.
3. Answers will vary.

Test-Taking Skills

2. A　　　3. C　　　4. B

Answer Pages

Page 74

Direct Activity

2. loaves　　　　**3.** shelves

Writing Practice

calves, elves

Stories will vary, with plurals circled.

Test-Taking Skills

2. C　　　　**3.** A　　　　**4.** C

Page 75

Direct Activity

2. foot—feet

3. mouse—mice

Writing Practice

Answers may vary.

Test-Taking Skills

2. B　　　　**3.** A　　　　**4.** C

Page 76

Direct Activity

2. piles
3. thieves
4. chairs
5. feet
6. children
7. deer
8. safes
9. geese
10. pens
11. womans
12. worries

13. storyes
14. mice
15. sheep
16. teeth
17. calvs
18. berries
19. boxs
20. dishes

Mystery phrase answer

With three wishes I'd…

Page 77

Direct Activity

2. I will

3. we are

Writing Practice

2. isn't Sentences will vary, with a triangle around *isn't*.

3. she'll Sentences will vary, with a triangle around *she'll*.

Test-Taking Skills

2. D　　　　**3.** A　　　　**4.** B

Page 78

Direct Activity

2. do not　　　　**3.** would not

Writing Practice

2. hasn't Sentences will vary, with a rectangle around *hasn't*.

3. I'm Sentences will vary, with a rectangle around *I'm*.

Test-Taking Skills

2. A　　　　**3.** B　　　　**4.** A

　　www.summerbridgeactivities.com　　Phonics—Grade 3—RBP0253

Answer Pages

Page 79

Direct Activity

2. they had, or they would
3. she had, or she would

Writing Practice

2. you've Sentences will vary, with a triangle around *you've*.
3. didn't Sentences will vary, with a triangle around *didn't*.

Test-Taking Skills

2. A   3. D   4. D

Page 80

Direct Activity

2. that is, or that has
3. they have

Writing Practice

2. it's Sentences will vary, with a circle around *it's*.
3. weren't Sentences will vary, with a circle around *weren't*.

Test-Taking Skills

2. D   3. A   4. C

Page 81

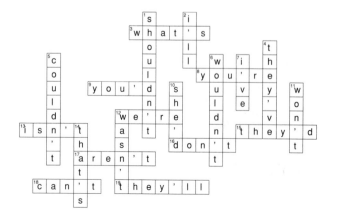

Page 82

Direct Activity

Start → can't → hasn't → they're → you've → I'm → wouldn't → she's → where's → doesn't → we've → I've → you'll → didn't → Finish.

Page 83

Direct Activity

2. mom's dress
3. frog's pond

Writing Practice

2. The (giraffe's) food is mostly hay.
3. (Adam's) video game is fun to play.

Test-Taking Skills

2. A   3. A   4. B

Page 84

Direct Activity

2. turtle's shell
3. table's chair

Writing Practice

2. This is (Shelby's) shoe.
3. This is (Mitchell's) plane.

Test-Taking Skills

2. B   3. B   4. A

Answer Pages

Page 85

Direct Activity
2. dogs' bones
3. cars' engines

Writing Practice
2. The (seals) beach balls are wet.
3. The (soldiers) uniforms are green.

Test-Taking Skills
2. B   3. B   4. A

Page 86

Direct Activity
2. bags' handles
3. lamps' shades

Writing Practice
2. The [books'] pages are numbered.
3. The [wagons'] wheels are all black.

Test-Taking Skills
2. A   3. B   4. B

Page 87

octopus's arms

dolphin's flippers

man's hat

boys' socks

Steve's train

frogs' guppies

dog's bones

door's lock

Wanda's rice

Mystery Message: Good work on this book's pages!

Page 88

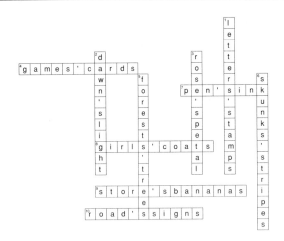

Page 89

Direct Activity
2. stew
3. pool

Writing Practice
2. Answers will vary, with *ew* word circled in sentence.
3. Answers will vary, with *oo* word circled in sentence.

Test-Taking Skills
2. A   3. B   4. D

Page 90

Direct Activity
2. br[ew], cr[ew], bl[ew]
3. t[oo]l, r[oo]m, sch[oo]l

Writing Practice
Sentences will vary, with rectangles around *oo* and *ew* words.

Test-Taking Skills
2. A   3. D   4. A

www.summerbridgeactivities.com   Phonics—Grade 3—RBP0253

Answer Pages

Page 91

Direct Activity

2. jaw

3. launch

Writing Practice

2. Answers will vary, with a circle around *aw* words.

3. Answers will vary, with a circle around *au* words.

Test-Taking Skills

2. A   3. D   4. A

Page 92

Direct Activity

2. dr(aw)

3. c(au)ght

Writing Practice

Sentences will vary, with *au* and *aw* words circled.

Test-Taking Skills

2. D   3. A   4. D

Page 93

Direct Activity

2. boil

3. oyster

Writing Practice

2. Sentences will vary, with *oi* word circled.

3. Sentences will vary, with *oy* word circled.

Test-Taking Skills

2. C   3. A   4. B

Page 94

Direct Activity

2. n o i s e   t o y

3. j o i n   j o y

Writing Practice

Sentences will vary, with *oi* and *oy* words circled.

Test-Taking Skills

2. C   3. D   4. B

Page 95

Direct Activity

2. house

3. flour

Writing Practice

2-3. Answers will vary, with a rectangle around *ou* words in the sentences.

Test-Taking Skills

2. B   3. A   4. B

Page 96

Direct Activity

2. hook

3. cook

Writing Practice

2. Answers will vary, with a rectangle around *oo* words in the sentence.

3. Answers will vary, with a rectangle around *oo* words in the sentence.

Test-Taking Skills

2. C   3. A   4. D

Phonics—Grade 3—RBP0253   www.summerbridgeactivities.com   ©RBP Books

Answer Pages

Page 97

Direct Activity

2. cl(ow)n bl(ow) cr(ow)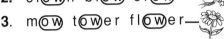
3. m(ow) t(ow)er fl(ow)er

Writing Practice

Answers will vary, with triangles around *ow* words.

Test-Taking Skills

2. A   3. B   4. D

Page Page 98

Direct Activity

2. tray   3. veil

Writing Practice

2. Answers will vary, with a triangle around the *ai* word in the sentence.
3. Answers will vary, with a triangle around the *ay* word in the sentence.

Test-Taking Skills

2. B   3. B   4. A

Page 99

Direct Activity

2. fl(ea) t(ea)
3. p(ee)l f(ee)l f(ee)t

Writing Practice

Answers will vary, with circles around *ea* and *ee* words in the story.

Test-Taking Skills

2. B   3. B   4. D

Page 100

Direct Activity

2. shoulder   3. boat

Writing Practice

2. Answers will vary, with the *ou* word circled in the sentence.
3. Answers will vary, with the *oa* word circled in the sentence.

Test-Taking Skills

2. A   3. B   4. B

Page Page 101

Direct Activity

2. young——————touch
3. wouldn't——————should

Writing Practice

Answers will vary, with rectangles around *ou* words in the story.

Test-Taking Skills

2. C   3. B   4. B

© RBP Books   www.summerbridgeactivities.com   Phonics—Grade 3—RBP0253

Page 102

Students should have 20 of the following:

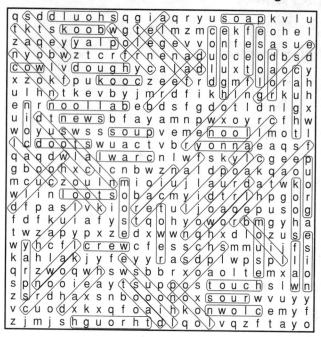

Page 103

Direct Activity

2. st\[ar\]   3. \[ar\]tist
2. mb   3. mb

Writing Practice

Sentences will vary, with rectangles around *ar* words.

Test-Taking Skills

2. B   3. C   4. C

Page 104

Direct Activity

2. (yard)   3. (car)

Writing Practice

Any knock-knock joke, with *ar* words circled.

Test-Taking Skills

2. C   3. B   4. A

Page 105

Direct Activity

2. b(i)rd   3. sh(i)rt

Writing Practice

2. \[girl\] Sentences will vary, with a rectangle around *girl*.
3. \[squirrel\] Sentences will vary, with a rectangle around *squirrel*.

Test-Taking Skills

2. C   3. C   4. B

Page 106

Direct Activity

2. dirt   3. squirrel

Writing Practice

Sentences will vary, with *ir* words circled.

Test-Taking Skills

2. B   3. A   4. B

Answer Pages

Page 107

Direct Activity
2. fern   3. water

Writing Practice
Sentences will vary, with triangles around the r-controlled parts of *er* words.

Test-Taking Skills
2. A   3. C   4. B

Page 108

Direct Activity
2. eraser   3. flower

Writing Practice
Any knock-knock joke, with *er* words circled.

Test-Taking Skills
2. B   3. A   4. B

Page 109

Direct Activity
2. turtle   3. burn

Writing Practice
2. purse Sentences will vary, with *purse* circled.
3. hurt Sentences will vary, with *hurt* circled.

Test-Taking Skills
2. A   3. B   4. C

Page 110

Direct Activity
2. fur   3. nurse

Writing Practice
Sentences will vary, with ur words circled.

Test-Taking Skills
2. B   3. C   4. A

Page 111

Direct Activity
2. horn   3. fork

Writing Practice
Sentences will vary, with a rectangle around the *or* parts of words.

Test-Taking Skills
2. C   3. C   4. A

Page 112

Direct Activity
2. storm   3. sports

Writing Practice
Any knock-knock joke, with *or* words circled.

Test-Taking Skills
2. C   3. B   4. B

www.summerbridgeactivities.com   Phonics—Grade 3—RBP0253

Answer Pages

Page 114

Direct Activity

1. C
2. Something like: Popcorn clouds are the largest, fluffiest, and roundest clouds in the sky.
3. Something like: The sleek, coiled, and feather-like clouds don't work well for shape finding.
4. tools
5. Answers will vary: about, afternoon, air, cartoon, caught, clouds, coiled, coolest, could, crew, day, disappearing, drawings, easy, enjoy, feather, fought, found, friends, good, great(est), group, hear, joined, lawn, leaping, loads, looking, loosen, need, news, roundest, rows, sleek, soon, team, too, tools, would, you, your.
6. Answers will vary: afternoon, air, are, art, cartoon, characters, curly, dark, disappearing, drawings, ever, feather, for, hear, horses, large, largest, park, part, popcorn, summer, super, there, together, very, wander, warm, wondered, work, worry, yard, your

Page 115

Direct Activity

2. untie
3. unlock

Writing Practice

2. unstitch Sentences will vary.
3. dislike Sentences will vary.

Test-Taking Skills

2. C   3. A   4. A

Page 116

Direct Activity

2. rewind   3. retry

Writing Practice

2. retrace Sentences will vary, with a rectangle around the *re* prefix.
3. reinvent Sentences will vary, with a rectangle around the *re* prefix.

Test-Taking Skills

2. B   3. A   4. A

Page 117

Direct Activity

2. presoak
3. pretest

Writing Practice

2. precook Sentences will vary, with a triangle around the *pre* prefix.
3. preslice Sentences will vary, with a triangle around the *pre* prefix.

Test-Taking Skills

2. B   3. A   4. C

Page 118

Direct Activity

2. overeat   3. oversleep

Writing Practice

2. overdo Sentences will vary, with a circle around the prefix *over*.
3. overload Sentences will vary, with a triangle around the prefix *over*.

Test-Taking Skills

2. A   3. C   4. A

Answer Pages

Page 119

Direct Activity

2. mistreat

3. misunderstand

Writing Practice

2. mislead Sentences will vary, with the prefix *mis* circled.

3. misplace Sentences will vary, with the prefix *mis* circled.

Test-Taking Skills

2. A   3. B   4. C

Page 120

Activity

discolor

resave

unbend

repaint

overcook

misfile

uncover

unwrap

redraw

oversleep

Mystery Message: There's no mistake, you are discovering the answers!

Page 121

Direct Activity

2. thoughtful

3. thankful

Writing Practice

2. wonderful Sentences will vary, with a rectangle around the suffix *ful*.

3. careful Sentences will vary, with a rectangle around the suffix *ful*.

Test-Taking Skills

2. A   3. B   4. B

Page 122

Direct Activity

2. homeless   3. cloudless

Writing Practice

2. colorless Sentences will vary, with a circle around the suffix *less*.

3. sleepless Sentences will vary, with a rectangle around the suffix *less*.

Test-Taking Skills

2. C   3. B   4. B

Page 123

Direct Activity

2. slowly

3. lucky

Writing Practice

2. mighty Sentences will vary, with a circle around the suffix *y*.

3. softly Sentences will vary, with a circle around the suffix *ly*.

Test-Taking Skills

2. A   3. B   4. A

www.summerbridgeactivities.com   Phonics—Grade 3—RBP0253

Page 124

Direct Activity

2. teachable
3. readable

Writing Practice

2. stackable Sentences will vary, with a circle around *stackable*.
3. likable Sentences will vary, with a circle around *likable*.

Test-Taking Skills

2. A   3. A   4. C

Page 125

Direct Activity

2. childish
3. yellowish

Writing Practice

2. babyish Sentences will vary, with a circle around *babyish*.
3. reddish Sentences will vary, with a circle around *reddish*.

Test-Taking Skills

2. A   3. A   4. A

Page 126

Activity

wishful

peaceful

washable

brownish

meaningless

vibrantly

thoughtless

powerful

odorless

cloudy

Mystery Message: Wonderful! You solved this so neatly!

Page 128

Direct Activity

1. D
2. Something like: The first three things from the story that you need to make a rainbow are freshly gathered light, an uncut piece of sky, and a large seamless bucket.
3. Something like: The last three things you need to do before your rainbow is ready are gently hang it across a clothesline, lightly mist it with spray, and allow it to re-dry.
4. clothesline
5. Answers may vary: disappears, discoloring, dissolve, misplace, overflowing, overlay, overnight, presoak, pretest, recut, re-dry, release, reset, resoak, unbreakable, uncover, uncovered, uncut, unlock, unwrapped
6. Answers may vary: bluish, carefully, directly, feathery, fluffy, freshly, gently, greenish, lightly, newly, orangish, purplish, reddish, roundish, seamless, slowly, unbreakable, usable, yellowish

Phonics—Grade 3—RBP0253

Answer Pages

Page 129

Direct Activity

2. flower—bed
3. flag—pole

Writing Practice

2. air/port Answers will vary.
3. cook/book Answers will vary.

Test-Taking Skills

2. A   3. B   4. B

Page 130

Direct Activity

2. tooth—brush
3. tea—pot

Writing Practice

2. foot/print Answers will vary.
3. fire/hose Answers will vary.

Test-Taking Skills

2. A   3. B   4. A

Page 131

Direct Activity

2. father, 2
3. city, 2

Writing Practice

Answers will vary.

Test-Taking Skills

2. A   3. B   4. B

Page 132

Direct Activity

2. raindrop, 2
3. toothbrush, 2

Writing Practice

Answers will vary.

Test-Taking Skills

2. A   3. B   4. A

Page 133

Direct Activity

2. butterfly, 3
3. can, 1

Writing Practice

Answers will vary.

Test-Taking Skills

2. A   3. C   4. D

Page 134

Direct Activity

2. skyscraper, 3
3. ring, 1

Writing Practice

Answers will vary.

Test-Taking Skills

2. C   3. B   4. A

Answer Pages

Page 135

Direct Activity
2. television, 4
3. piano, 3

Writing Practice
Answers will vary.

Test-Taking Skills
2. A   3. C   4. A

Page 136

Direct Activity
Start ⟶ alligator ⟶ mouse ⟶ kitchen ⟶ automobile ⟶ heal ⟶ shoelace ⟶ tie ⟶ remote ⟶ pocket ⟶ money ⟶ watch ⟶ paper ⟶ Finish!

Page 137

Direct Activity
2. cat, 3
3. ball, 2

Writing Practice
eggs, flour, milk, oranges, raisins and sugar.

Test-Taking Skills
2. C   3. C   4. B

Page 138

Direct Activity
1. television, 3
2. chair, 1
3. doughnut, 2

Writing Practice
cleaning, dinner, errands, exercises, housework, and laundry.

Test-Taking Skills
2. B   3. C   4. A

Page 139

Direct Activity
1. hoop, 3
2. car, 1
3. hat, 2

Writing Practice
ball, bow, box, dog, doll, and dress.

Test-Taking Skills
2. B   3. A   4. B

Page 140

Direct Activity
1. mitten, 2
2. mountain, 3
3. map, 1

Writing Practice
leaves, lilacs, lilies, thorns, trees, and tulips.

Test-Taking Skills
2. C   3. B   4. B

Phonics—Grade 3--RBP0253   www.summerbridgeactivities.com   ©RBP Books

Page 141

Direct Activity

1. bat, 3
2. barn, 2
3. ball, 1

Writing Practice

periwinkle, pine-green, pink, plum, puce and purple.

Test-Taking Skills

2. A   3. B   4. A

Page 142

Direct Activity

2. blue
3. brown
4. gray
5. green
6. orange
7. pink
8. purple
9. red
10. yellow

Page 143

Direct Activity

2. open, close
3. happy, sad

Writing Practice

2. Mike will (close) the doors at five o'clock.
3. The car is going (down) the hill.

Test-Taking Skills

2. C   3. A   4. D

Page 144

Direct Activity

2. hot, cold
3. sweet, sour

Writing Practice

2. Jacob was (asleep) when I went downstairs.
3. Please turn to the (front) of the room.

Test-Taking Skills

2. B   3. C   4. B

Page 145

Direct Activity

2. film, movie
3. flower, blossom

Writing Practice

2. Did you see that [fast] runner?
3. Will you [clean] the clothes in the hamper?

Test-Taking Skills

2. D   3. B   4. A

Page 146

Direct Activity

2. small, little
3. sofa, couch

Writing Practice

2. I love to make the baby [smile]
3. Be careful not to [harm] yourself.

Test-Taking Skills

2. C   3. C   4. D

Answer Pages

Page 147

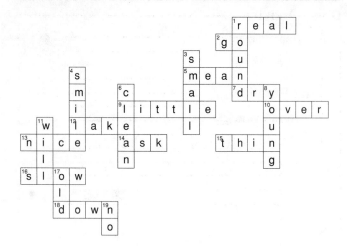

Page 148

Direct Activity

1. p~~oo~~r
2. ~~go~~
3. (fire)
4. h~~a~~te
5. (still)
6. ~~cr~~azy
7. (dark)
8. (light)
9. (asleep)
10. st~~e~~al
11. fa~~s~~t
12. (slow)
13. (wet)
14. (untrue)
15. (never)
16. (shut)
17. (yes)
18. (before)
19. (bumpy)
20. (after)

Mystery Phrase: Is the antonym for pickles sweet or sour?

Page 149

Direct Activity

2. sun, son
3. cot, caught

Writing Practice

2. Answers will vary, with homophones circled in sentence.
3. Answers will vary, with homophones circled in sentence.

Test-Taking Skills

2. A   3. B   4. C

Page 150

Direct Activity

2. Answers will vary.
3. Answers will vary.

Writing Practice

2. Any sentence using the word *beet* or *beat*.
3. Any sentence using the word *heal* or *heel*.

Test-Taking Skills

2. C   3. A   4. B

Page 151

Direct Activity

2. wind, wind
3. close, close

Writing Practice

2. the sound a dog makes, the wood on a tree trunk
3. to show the way, a kind of metal

Test-Taking Skills

2. A   3. A   4. A

Answer Pages

Page 152

Direct Activity

2. Answers will vary.

3. Answers will vary.

Writing Practice

2. fine Answers will vary, with a rectangle around the homograph in the sentence.

3. box Answers will vary, with a rectangle around the homograph in the sentence.

Test-Taking Skills

2. B   3. A   4. B

Page 154

Direct Activity

1. C

2. Something like: Three things that Sun Black did when the giants told her that she had to leave are she turned pale, cried buckets of tears, and wiped them with the tears in her dress.

3. Something like: The giants found Sun Black when they came to their mansion. Sun Black was putting dirt on their dishes and making oatmeal for dinner.

4. tasty candy

5. sun, needed, night, pale, their, threw, made

6. while the wind made the trees wind around in circles, cried buckets of tears and wiped them with the tears in her dress, fence while standing on fences.

Page 155

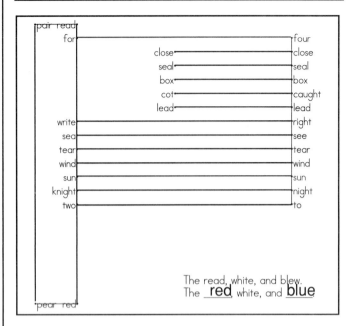

The read, white, and blew.
The __red__, white, and **blue**

Page 156

Direct Activity

Words crossed off: crown, hut, mall, quack, quaint, vampire, and walrus

absent / crow – ant, brick, butter, cream

crumb / hover – cut, dent, flip, hot

ice / lucky – icicle, kangaroo, lamp, lost

man / put – map, nest, owl, push

quick / stun– quiet, rake, stop, stuck

Page 157

Direct Activity

1. p. 12   11. p. 28
2. p. 28   12. p. 12
3. p. 1   13. p. 28
4. p. 34   14. p. 1
5. p. 39   15. p. 34
6. p. 39   16. p. 12
7. p. 1   17. p. 34
8. p. 28   18. p. 1
9. p. 39   19. p. 39
10. p. 12   20. p. 34

www.summerbridgeactivities.com   Phonics—Grade 3—RBP0253

Practice writing below.

𝒜 𝒶

ℬ 𝒷

𝒞

𝒞

𝒟

𝒹

ℰ

𝑒

Practice writing below.

$\mathcal{F}$

f

$\mathcal{G}$

g

$\mathcal{H}$

h

$\mathcal{L}$

i

$\mathcal{J}$

j

www.summerbridgeactivities.com Phonics—Grade 3—RBP0253

Practice writing below.

K

k

L

l

M

m

N

n

O

O

Practice writing below.

p

p

2

q

R

r

S

s

T

t

www.summerbridgeactivities.com   Phonics—Grade 3—RBP0253

Practice writing below.

$\mathcal{U}$

$\mathcal{U}$

$\mathcal{V}$

v

$\mathcal{U}$

w

χ

x

$\mathcal{Y}$ y

z z

Phonics—Grade 3—RBP0253

www.summerbridgeactivities.com   ©RBP Books